Communications in Computer and Information Science 654

Commenced Publication in 2007
Founding and Former Series Editors:
Phoebe Chen, Alfredo Cuzzocrea, Xiaoyong Du, Orhun Kara, Ting Liu,
Krishna M. Sivalingam, Dominik Ślęzak, Takashi Washio, Xiaokang Yang,
and Junsong Yuan

More information about this series at http://www.springer.com/series/7899

Andreas Holzinger · Hugo Plácido Silva ·
Markus Helfert (Eds.)

Computer-Human Interaction Research and Applications

First International Conference, CHIRA 2017
Funchal, Madeira, Portugal, October 31 – November 2, 2017
Revised Selected Papers

 Springer

Editors
Andreas Holzinger ⓘ
Medical University Graz
Graz, Austria

Hugo Plácido Silva
IT- Institute of Telecommunications
Lisbon, Portugal

Markus Helfert
Dublin City University
Dublin, Ireland

ISSN 1865-0929   ISSN 1865-0937   (electronic)
Communications in Computer and Information Science
ISBN 978-3-030-32964-8   ISBN 978-3-030-32965-5   (eBook)
https://doi.org/10.1007/978-3-030-32965-5

This Springer imprint is published by the registered company Springer Nature Switzerland AG
The registered company address is: Gewerbestrasse 11, 6330 Cham, Switzerland

Preface

The present book includes extended and revised versions of a set of selected papers from the International Conference on Computer-Human Interaction Research and Applications (CHIRA 2017), held in Funchal, Madeira, Portugal, during October 31 – November 2, 2017.

CHIRA 2017 received 35 paper submissions from 22 countries, of which 20% were included in this book.

The papers were selected by the event chairs and their selection was based on a number of criteria that included the classifications and comments provided by the Program Committee members, the session chairs' assessment, and also the program chairs' global view of all papers included in the technical program. The authors of selected papers were then invited to submit a revised and extended version of their papers having at least 30% novel material.

The purpose of CHIRA is to bring together professionals, academics, and students who are interested in the advancement of research and practical applications of human-technology and human-computer interaction.

Papers describing original work on advanced methods, prototypes, systems, tools and techniques, as well as general survey papers indicating future directions were presented at the conference.

The papers selected to be included in this book contribute to the understanding of relevant trends of current research on Computer-Human Interaction, including interaction design, human factors, entertainment, cognition, perception, user-friendly software and systems, pervasive technologies, and interactive devices.

We would like to thank all the authors for their contributions and also the reviewers who have helped ensure the quality of this publication.

October 2017

Andreas Holzinger
Hugo Plácido Silva
Markus Helfert

Organization

Conference Chair

Markus Helfert — Dublin City University, Ireland

Program Co-chairs

Hugo Plácido Silva — Institute of Telecommunications (IT), Portugal
Andreas Holzinger — Medical University Graz, Austria

Program Committee

Alessandra Agostini	University of Milano-Bicocca, Italy
David Ahlström	Alpen-Adria-Universität Klagenfurt, Austria
Ahmad Taher Azar	Benha University, Egypt
Paul Baker	Georgia Institute of Technology, USA
Martin Baumann	Ulm University, Germany
Christine Chauvin	Université de Bretagne Sud, France
Ahyoung Choi	Gachon University, South Korea
Yang-Wai Chow	University of Wollongong, Australia
Lewis Chuang	Max Planck Institute for Biological Cybernetics, Germany
Cesar Collazos	Universidad del Cauca, Colombia
Pierre De Loor	Lab-STICC Laboratory, France
Lizette De Wet	University of the Free State, South Africa
Paramartha Dutta	Visva-Bharati University, India
Vania Estrela	Universidade Federal Fluminense, Brazil
Ronak Etemadpour	City College, CUNY, USA
Peter Forbrig	University of Rostock, Germany
Diego Gachet	European University of Madrid, Spain
Kiel Gilleade	USA
Abby Goodrum	Wilfrid Laurier University, Canada
Toni Granollers	University of Lleida, Spain
Karin Harbusch	Universität Koblenz-Landau, Germany
Bruno Heberlin	EPFL, Switzerland
Martin Hitz	Alpen-Adria-Universität Klagenfurt, Austria
Andreas Holzinger	Medical University Graz, Austria
Sylwia Hyniewska	World Hearing Centre, Poland
Victor Kaptelinin	Umeå University, Sweden
Roland Kaschek	CSB-System AG, Germany
Adi Katz	Shamoon College of Engineering (SCE), Israel
Simeon Keates	University of Greenwich, UK

Suzanne Kieffer	Université Catholique de Louvain, Belgium
Bernd Korn	German Aerospace Center, Germany
Youquan Liu	Chang'an University, China
Arminda Lopes	Madeira Interactive Technologies Institute (Miti) and Instituto Politecnico de Castelo Branco, Portugal
Wendy Lucas	Bentley University, USA
Robert Macredie	Brunel University London, UK
Gerrit Meixner	Heilbronn University, Germany
Daniel Mestre	Aix-Marseille University, CNRS, France
Max Mulder	TU Delft, The Netherlands
Jaime Muñoz-Arteaga	Universidad Autónoma de Aguascalientes (UAA), Mexico
Radoslaw Niewiadomski	University of Genoa, Italy
Michael O'Grady	University College Dublin, Ireland
Yoosoo Oh	Daegu University, South Korea
Meltem Ozturan	Bogazici University, Turkey
Gianluca Paravati	Polytechnic University of Turin, Italy
Lyn Pemberton	University of Brighton, UK
Sheng-Lung Peng	National Dong Hwa University, Taiwan
Claudio Pinhanez	IBM Research, Brazil
Nitendra Rajput	IBM Research (New Delhi), India
Laura Ripamonti	Università degli Studi di Milano, Italy
Paul Rosenthal	Germany
Andrea Sanna	Politecnico di Torino, Italy
João Sequeira	Instituto Superior Técnico, Portugal
Jean Vanderdonckt	Université Catholique de Louvain, Belgium
Spyros Vosinakis	University of the Aegean, Greece
Sven Wachsmuth	Bielefeld University, Germany
Marcus Winter	University of Brighton, UK
Lixuan Zhang	Weber State University, USA

Additional Reviewers

| Marius Koller | Heilbronn University, Germany |
| Paulina Paluch | World Hearing Center, Poland |

Invited Speakers

Larry Constantine	M-ITI, USA
Chris Csíkszentmihályi	M-ITI, Portugal
Gerrit van der Veer	Vrije Universiteit Amsterdam (VUA), The Netherlands
Max Mulder	TU Delft, The Netherlands

Contents

Personality Archetypes, Pantomime, Comics: New Methods to Design Interfaces with Human Traits

Claudio Pinhanez[✉]

IBM Research, São Paulo, SP 04007-900, Brazil
csantosp@br.ibm.com

Abstract. This paper addresses the issue of designing interfaces which have human traits and behaviors, proposing that they have to satisfy three basic requirements: the human traits must be coherent, there should be mechanisms specific to deal with conflict with the user, and they have to handle dramatic situations created by the user. To support the design process to meet these three requirements, four design methods are presented, using frameworks and techniques used in social psychology, theater, comics, and movie animation. The design methods work towards better definition of the human personality to be perceived by the user; unearthing and mitigating the main conflicts and associated emotions to be handled by the interface; creating a rich representation of the dramatized interaction and using it to explore the space of design solutions; and transforming into interface actions the solutions found through theatrical methods. We exemplify and illustrate the design methods with results from three student workshops in the context of designing a service recovery interface for e-commerce.

Keywords: Personified interfaces · Design methods · Chatbots · Humanoid robots

1 Introduction

In the science fiction world, it has been common to see computers and robots with rich human traits such as personalities, intentions, human-like conversational abilities, and (sometimes evil) emotions. Complex computer personalities and even robot psychiatry are present in the most important stories of Isaac Asimov and Arthur C. Clarke, and often personified computers are the main stars of works of Ray Bradbury and Philip Dick. In the movies, several episodes of *Star Trek* in the 1960s dealt with vengeful machines and dysfunctional robots, while *HAL 9000* tried to kill astronauts to assure a successful mission in *2001*. Movies and TV series with friendly and evil computers have been a staple since then, including the cute and funny *R2D2* and *C3PO* of the *Star Wars* saga, the vengeful pleasure robots of *WestWorld*, and the chilling, sexy, and terrifying *Ava* of *Ex Machina* which transforms a Turing Test into a terror nightmare.

In almost all of those cases, the computer (or robot) interacts using natural language with its human counterparts and exhibits human traits either in the way it talks or performs actions. In many ways, those *Sci-Fi* creations have imprinted an imaginary

© Springer Nature Switzerland AG 2019
A. Holzinger et al. (Eds.): CHIRA 2017, CCIS 654, pp. 1–19, 2019.
https://doi.org/10.1007/978-3-030-32965-5_1

perception that smart computers will be able not only to converse with their users but will do it while exhibiting rich character personalities and complex acting behaviors.

Moving away from science fiction and into reality, we are witnessing since the beginning of the 2010s that computer interfaces based on speech, chat, and avatars are starting to become more available and common. With the presence of *Apple's Siri* and *Microsoft's Cortana* in our smartphones and computers, and the emergence of voice-activated home devices such as *Amazon's Echo* and *Google Home*, smart talkative computers are now part of the reality of billions of users worldwide. At the same time, with the explosion of neural network-based natural language processing *(NLP)* in the 2010s, speech- and text-based chatbots of all kinds and purposes have left the laboratories and have become a part of people's daily conversations. With cloud-based *Artificial Intelligence (AI)* services such as *IBM Watson Conversation Services* available at the fingertips of developers, interacting with customers using an artificial conversational system became a standard offer of most large consumer companies. At the same time, the first prototypes of conversational humanoid robots are being put in direct contact with customers, using platforms such as *Aldebaran's Nao* and *Pepper*, conversational toys, and many on-board automotive systems.

In most of those cases, the computer interfaces exhibit some degree of typical human traits such as personality, gender, sentiments, and even, in some cases, the appearance of consciousness. Research since the 1990s has shown that there is almost always some level of humanization in any interaction with computers [1], even in the simplest cases of terminal, green text-based interaction. But with the recent availability of speech understanding and production, chatting capabilities, and humanoid embodiments, the users' reading of human traits in computers is likely to have greatly increased. Anecdotally they seem to have trigger behaviors from users resembling those used to deal with other human beings. Users greet, thank, yell at, mock, curse, and play with those interfaces in a way resembling some of the typical interactions depicted in sci-fi stories and movies, even in the cases where the computer capabilities are very limited [2].

There is, however, a huge gap between the imaginary created by science fiction and the reality of today's intelligent systems. Current technology is far from creating the kind of sentient being we have seen in movies: most conversational systems are still created using manual scripting of the uttered text and the depicted emotions. Nevertheless, some level of user perception of computer humanity is already present in those interfaces [3], and there is very little guidance available on how to design the interface elements, such as text, appearance, and emotions, so the conversational system displays human traits with are coherent with the tasks being performed with the computer.

Most of the guidance in the literature is of practical nature [4, 5] and some of the related theoretical discussion [6] predates considerably the reality of current technology. The goal of this paper is to explore ways to bridge both the theoretical and practical gaps in the design of computer interfaces which display human-like behaviors (such as conversing) and, doing so, exhibit perceivable human traits such as personality, gender, and character. The theoretical framework presented here is adapted and expanded from some previous work done in the context of service design [7], which advocated the emergence of human traits in people's relationship with service providers and explored some new design methodology in the context of service conflict resolution. Later, we reformulated this theoretical structure and adapted it to the context of interfaces with human traits [8], considering fundamental requirements and examining theoretical frameworks, notably from Sociology, Psychology, and the Arts, which could support the design process of such interfaces with human traits. This exploration led us to propose four design methods which have been explored in three workshops with students, briefly described in [8].

We start this paper by revisiting the discussion presented in [8] about the main requirements which distinguish the design of such interfaces from traditional interfaces. In particular, we reiterate that interfaces with human traits (1) must exhibit behaviors which are coherent with everyday human behaviors and traits, (2) must deal with conflict with their users, and (3) must be able to handle drama. Following, we do a brief review of the theoretical frameworks proposed in [8] to support the design of the human traits of the personified interface and its embodiment, personality, and social behaviors; and to enable the interface to manage conflict and fulfil dramatic roles. We then present and discuss in more detail the four design methods described summarily in [8], which are similar to some of the ones originally proposed in [7]. However, unlike in those two previous works, we explore here in detail the processes and results of three design workshops. Although those workshops were originally conducted to design human traits for a web interface of a service provider, the results obtained exemplify quite well the methods proposed, and are absolutely relevant to the context of this paper. Designing the human traits of a web-based service recovery system is simply a special case of designing an interface with human traits as we will discuss later in more detail.

The main focus of this paper is to discuss how new design methods can support the creation of rich, meaningful, and trustable interactions with the user in the context of systems which elicit perception of human traits and behaviors from their users. This is not a trivial task since human beings are extremely sensitive (in the negative sense) to creatures or systems which look like human beings but fail to behave adequately. We have seen many instances of intelligent systems which have been designed portraying something like a caricature of a human being. In many cases, such systems are perceived simply as being cute as toys are, but there have been instances where fails in the design of human traits and behaviors deeply annoyed their users. This was the case of *Clippy*, the infamous interface character introduced in *Microsoft Office* in the 1990s, whose disastrous deployment possibly delayed similar projects for two decades.

2 Personified Interfaces

We use the term *personified interfaces* to describe interfaces which display human traits such as personality, gender, and character; and the term *personified machines* to name the systems which employ personified interfaces. Notice that personified interfaces tend to elicit typical human-to-human behaviors from their users which are not necessarily seen in traditional interfaces.

Principles and practices used today in interface design implicitly assume that users are not interacting with personified machines but with a traditional computer. It is a fundamental proposition of this paper that personified interfaces tend new requirements given that their users expect some level of "humanness". We encapsulate those in three fundamental requirements we believe most personified interfaces need to meet:

1. personified interfaces must exhibit <u>coherent</u> human traits and social behaviors;
2. personified interfaces must be able to deal with <u>conflict</u> with their users;
3. personified interfaces must handle <u>dramatic</u> narratives created by their users.

Providing empirical evidence of the validity of each of the three requirements is beyond the scope of this paper. We treat here those three requirements as our working hypotheses. We acknowledge that this validation is needed and we believe those hypotheses can and should be tested using methods such as structured interviews, focus groups, user surveys, and experiments similar to the ones described in [1]. Nevertheless, in our practice with interface and service design professionals, most of them found the three requirements relevant and agreed that they are likely to be present in most scenarios of personified interfaces. The most important feedback we got from designers has been a desire to know how those requirements can be met by the design process.

If personified machines need to have coherent human traits, deal well with conflict, and handle drama, to what extent the personified interface must be constructed to be perceived as an "artificial" human being, that is, how much do they need to personify the interface? Which are the human traits and characteristics more often perceived and are needed by the users? When and how do users treat—and would like to treat—personified machines with courtesy? How to design interfaces which highlight particularly desirable human traits? How can the interface drive the drama behind the interaction process constructed by the user and better participate in it?

We postulate here that adequately designing the *interface persona* is a fundamental part of the process of the personified interfaces, where here we use the term *interface persona* to mean the combination of the personified interface's visual appearance, its style of speaking and writing, its action and emotive affordances, and the internal processes which are responsible for generating and controlling the behavior of the interface. Simply, the interface persona is the set of interface affordances and features which create the perception of humanness of the interface, which must also be the object of a targeted design process using specific design methods such as those described in Sect. 4. This paper looks deeply into those methods for designing interface personas, but first it is necessary to understand further the ideas and concepts behind the three requirements.

2.1   Coherent Human Traits

Research and practice have proven that users have a strong tendency to attribute human characteristics to objects, places, and machines, and change interaction patterns accordingly [1]. Notably when machines engage their users with voice or text, users have shown to recognize gender, personality, and race [3], even when explicitly remembered that they are interacting with machines. People act as if they just cannot avoid seeing a human being in whatever speaks or moves like a person, as movie animations and puppetry easily remind us. Beyond that, users of conversational systems exhibit social behaviors with machines typically associated with other human beings, such as similarity attraction [9]. For instance, Lee et al. [10] created an experiment in which male users not only enjoyed more interacting with "male" computers than "female" computers, but also trusted them more (and vice-versa for female users).

At the same time, creating believable "human beings" can be a challenge, as bad acting in theatre and movies often reminds us. This has been shown in the context of machine interfaces by studies in which people react negatively when faced with a personified interface with incoherent human traits [11]. In another experiment, [12] subjects listened to descriptions of products recorded either by Caucasian Americans or first-generation Koreans, while being exposed to photos of Koreans and Caucasian Australians, alternatively. A photo of a Caucasian Australian with a Korean voice not only increased the dislike with the quality of the voice but also caused a less favorable rating of the products described. When the personified interface employs a visual, humanoid embodiment, such as in virtual humans or robots, adequate characterization of human traits is even more important [13, 14].

In most cases of interface design today, issues related to the human traits of personified interfaces are ignored by the design process. We describe later some design methods which can support the design of gender, race, level of schooling, personality, and other key human traits of a personified interface.

2.2 Dealing with Conflict

When a machine talks to a user or has a humanoid body, human beings have tendency to believe that the machine has its own intents and desires, and feel compelled to respond taking that fact in account [1]. Personified interfaces tend to intensify the adoption by their users of what Dennett calls the *intentional stance* [15], the ascription of intents and goals to a system people are interacting with.

The problem is that quite often the user's own intents and goals are not the same as the intents and goals that the users perceive, correctly or incorrectly, as being the goals of the personified machine. This is particularly common when using interfaces which provide services [7]. For example, a customer care chatbot tend to incarnate the goals of its corresponding organization and may try to do an upsell when the user wants to return a product. This gap between the goals of the user and the perceived goals of the machine/organization often breeds conflict, as much as it is common to see in encounters of customers and employees.

Some recent studies of today's conversational systems have identified many of those cases of conflict and frustration. Luger and Sellen [2], investigating *Apple's Siri*, report many cases where Siri's failures where perceived as stubbornness. We believe this is an intrinsic issue of personified interfaces, that machines are often perceived as in conflict with the user. User will often regard those machines as mean, stubborn, selfish, and arrogant, and will argue with them because they believe, sometimes correctly, that they are pursuing goals different from theirs. Conflict is inevitable, and designers should consider from the very start of the design process how it can be managed and, if possible, mitigated. Some of the design methods proposed later have the clear purpose of magnifying conflict so to facilitate the discovery of ways to handle it better.

2.3   Handling Drama

Beyond intentions and goals, people also have to understand how the different inter-actions they perform with other people make sense as a whole. For that, human beings often resort to represent those interactions to themselves as dramatic narratives [6]. They see their roles in their everyday life as heroes or victims and by rendering other people as gods or villains, it becomes much easier to figure out other people intentions, values, and goals, and most importantly, they can more easily predict the actions of other people. Narrative structures such as causation, succession, and counterpoint, facilitate and make manageable the representation of the complex patterns of our social life.

Using narratives as representations or cognitive foundations for human-machine interaction is not new to HCI theory as, for example, in Laurel's work on computer as theatre [6]. But it is reasonable to expect that in personified interfaces the use of narrative structures by the user easily becomes dramatic, since it is amplified by the human traits and conflict-laden encounters. Personified machines can easily become friends, gods, villains, or sidekicks in the narrative constructed by the user to cogni-tively represent her interaction with a personified machine.

This has been observed when users report their initial experiences with speech-based personal assistants [2], which sometimes becomes a story of high expectations and deceit. In their first encounter with *Siri* [2] they often ask difficult questions, get disappointed with basic mistakes, resort to ask for jokes or other form of play, and finally use it for menial tasks. Machines go from being oracles to idiots, then to jesters, and finally become servants. This can be mitigated by targeting those issues during the design process and proactively trying to break the construction of this first, disastrous narrative by moving quickly to teaching the user the assistant's capabilities.

Identification and handling of those dramatic structures is important in all inter-faces, but in personified interfaces it becomes a key requirement since personification tends to enhance the users' perception that the actions and responses of a personified machine are part of a greater story. Designers need to consider which narratives their users are likely to co-create to explain and represent their interactions with the machine. As seen later, our design methods provide ways to unearth those narratives and rep-resent them.

3   Supporting Theoretical Frameworks

Human beings are complex creatures and therefore we should not expect that designing interface personas and constructing effective personified interfaces to be a simple task. To address this challenge, the design process should be grounded as much as possible in solid theoretical frameworks which have been used in other disciplines to understand and, in some cases, "create" human beings (such as in theatre). Previous work [8] have dealt extensively with this issue, so here we present those theories briefly, to the extent that they are needed to understand the design methods described later. The reader is referred to [8] for a more detailed description.

Human Traits in Interaction: Extensive research has shown that users tend to assign human traits such as gender, personality, and emotions to computer systems [1].

For instance, Newman et al. [16] has shown that people perceive gender even in the absence of explicit cues, for instance, from the writing style. Gender is important because people have biases for specific genders to help them in specific tasks [17] and have similar reactions towards perceived race and place of origin in conversational systems [18]. On the other hand, many studies have shown that people with inconsistent personalities and traits are often perceived by their interlocutors as incapable, unpredictable, or liars, and similarly for conversational systems [3, 12]. Also, the studies on *similarity attraction* have shown that people like people who are similar to them [9, 19], and the same is also true for computer systems [20]. Therefore, in many cases there is not a right gender, race, or other human trait for a given system. Instead, they should match the corresponding traits in the user.

Stanislavski's System: Konstantin Stanislavski [21] departed from the traditional reliance in theatre on facial expressions, excessive gesturing, and voice manipulation. For Stanislavski, *"Acting is doing."*, actors perform actions which manifest their emotions and goals [21]. Our design methods adapt this concept to personified machines. For instance, a personified interface should not display a sad face in case of failures: regret is better expressed with acts of repair and renouncing, such as giving a voucher to compensate for a service failure.

Puppetry: Making audiences believe that there is an intelligent, emotional human being inside every puppet is part of the ancient and yet powerful collection of techniques of puppetry [22]. One key lesson from puppetry is to choose stories and roles which can be conveyed by the affordances of the puppet. For instance, hand puppets are not suited for narratives with long dialogues or which require facial expressions. At the same time, puppetry often relies on exposing the materials and inner workings of puppets, sometimes openly showcasing the puppeteer on the stage as in *bunraku* theatre (a traditional Japanese puppet art). Similarly, a personified interface may show, instead of hiding, its limitations and, paradoxically, increase the trust of the user in it as it is done with puppets.

Movie Animation: Similar challenges are faced when making a sequence of drawings convey emotions and humor. To deal with them, Walt Disney's animators in the 1930s compiled a set of 12 fundamental principles of animation, to create what they called *the illusion of life* [23]. For example, one of this principles is *anticipation*: *"Before Mickey reaches to grab an object, he first raises his arms as he stares at the article, broadcasting the fact that he is going to do something with that particular object."* [23], p. 52. In personified interfaces, we can apply anticipation by making sure that an important action is preceded by smaller actions which are likely to lead to it.

Personality Archetypes: There is a vast number of proposed personality models of human beings, among them *personality theory*, a general name for psychological models which assign archetypal categories of personality to human beings, aiming to help predict the effects of having each archetype in a context or how each archetype normally interacts with people of the other archetypes. In our design methods we have used the *Myers-Briggs Type Indicator* (MBTI) [24] which classifies individuals along four dichotomies: *Extraversion* vs. *Intraversion* (E-I), the preferred mode to acquire energy and motivation; *Sensing* vs. *iNtuition* (S-N), determining the preferred mode to obtain information; *Thinking* and *Feeling* (T-F), referring to the decision-making mechanism of choice; and *Judging* vs. *Perceiving* (J-P) indicating the preferred mode to relate to the world, using *T-F* or *S-N* channels, respectively. The four preferences define the 16 MBTI types: *ESTJ*, *ESTP*, and so on. We also have looked into *horoscope signs*, such as the *Sun sign* astrology (*Leo*, *Virgo*, etc.) which we regard simply as a compendium of 12 basic human archetypes. In many cultural contexts using horoscope signs is easier than other methods because many people are very familiar with them. For instance, a *Virgo* chatbot is easily understood as nurturing, patient, loving, and flexible.

Social Intrapersonal Phenomena: We also employ ideas from social psychology, particularly the study of *attitudes*, or basic likes and dislikes; *persuasion*; *social cognition*, or how people collect, process, and remember information about others; *self-concept*, or how people perceive themselves; and *cognitive dissonance*, the feeling that someone's behavior or self-concept are inconsistent. For instance, *cognitive dissonance* increases whenever people voluntarily do activities they dislike to achieve a goal. Paradoxically, doing this cause the perception of the value of the goal to be increased, as noticed in some studies on the use of voice-based personal assistants [2].

Social Interpersonal Phenomena: Many areas studied in social psychology are particularly relevant to the design of personified interfaces: *social influence*, or how conformity, compliance, and obedience manifest themselves; *interpersonal attraction*, including propinquity, familiarity, similarity, physical attractiveness, and social exchange; and *interpersonal perception*, which includes issues related to the accuracy, self-other agreement, similarity, projection, assumed similarity, reciprocity, etc. It is often true that the more someone interact with a person, the more likely she is to become emotionally engage with that person, or the *propinquity effect*. Personified systems used every day such as one-button smartphone assistants or always-on ubiquitous speakers, will tend to be better perceived and cared for by human beings.

Emotional Communication Theory: Several categorizations of emotion types have been proposed, including Ekman's basic set of emotions [25], *happiness, sadness, fear, surprise, anger,* and *disgust*. A more complete model is Plutchik's *sentiment wheel* [26] which adds *anticipation* and *trust* as basic emotions, describes variations of intensity in each emotion, and assigns colors to them.

4   Design Methods for Personified Interfaces

We are ready now to present some design methods we have developed to address the three requirements of personified interfaces: coherent human traits, conflict dealing, and handling drama. Traditional design methods used in computer-human interaction are also clearly applicable to personified interfaces, since there are many interface challenges which are solely related to human-computer communication issues. Therefore, for all purposes, we assume that the overall personified interface design process also applies concepts, methods, and steps of a typical user-centered design such as, for example, the construction of *user personas* [27].

We describe here four design methods: *personality workshop, conflict battle, comics workshop,* and *puppet prototyping.* They were inspired and are supported by the theoretical frameworks from social sciences, theater, puppetry, and social psychology discussed in Sect. 3.

The design methods are adapted from methods discussed in previous work on service design [7], and also briefly presented in [8]. They were originally developed to address issues in the design of computer interfaces to service systems, specifically the process of personification of the service provider which often occurs during service recovery. Service recovery is often a very conflicting process where users see themselves battling against (personified) corporations. With the growing availability and popularity of personal assistants, chatbots, and humanoid robots, we revisited those methods in this paper but within the larger context of personified interfaces.

4.1 The Three Test Workshops

The four service design methods were explored and further developed in three workshops with students in the context of designing the service recovery interface for a self-service e-commerce website. We discuss and show results of those workshops in this paper because they do a great job in exemplifying the methods and the kind of results we are seeking. The workshops were conducted in distinct locations and in different contexts. The first workshop was executed in a service design school with about 10 service design students in three sessions of 4 h. The other two workshops were shorter, conducted in one day each involving 2 groups of 15 students, mostly from computer science backgrounds. All the results shown in this paper are from the first workshop.

The service design workshops started with participants being presented with the problem of designing the service recovery interface of a e-commerce delivery failure system for a non-existing small website for sneakers. This was supposed to be a small company with a single warehouse which does all its transactions through its website, e-mail system, and a courier service. As part of the input to the participants, a list of *user personas*, representative of the typical customers of the sneaker store was provided (see Table 1), as well as a list of typical service failures such as failing to deliver the product, the product was incorrect or had defects, etc. Following, we provided the participants a brief description of how the company worked and the its key stakeholders.

Participants were then led to address the problem of designing the interface of a web-based delivery failure system for that company. The key change being demanded was the automation of the delivery failure process which was handled solely by e-mail exchanges with an employee. An important constraint is that the company did not have and did not want to operate a call-center service for service delivery recovery.

The following *list of usecases* of service failure was provided to the participants:

- Nothing was delivered.
- An incorrect product (color, size, model) was shipped.
- The shipped product had defects.
- The customer did not like the product and returned it.

Table 1. Customer *personas* used in the test workshops, with 4 typical customers including a *service challenger*, Blake.

MELVIN	PATRICIA
Startup CEO; 33-year old; male; likes to show off new sneakers; quality is important; limited time; color-blind; does not tolerate bad service	High-school sophomore; 14-year old; female; middle-class parents; fashion-obsessed; has difficult making decisions; impatient
AUDREY	BLAKE
Mother of adolescent kids; 45-years old; buys sneakers for kids; lots of free time; not well versed on adolescent trends; good writer; limited web skills	Brick-and-mortar sneaker store owner; 56-year old; male; buy-and-return sneakers to support his own store; knows all tricks of the trade

4.2   The Personality Workshop

The first of the proposed methods, called *personality workshop*, is where designers, potential users, and stakeholders try to establish the main human characteristics of a personified interface and, in particular, its personality. Participants explore individually and in group the personality traits of the interface by using the *Myers-Briggs* framework. To accomplish this, they fill in a table containing typical service failures as rows and the user personas as columns. For each cell, they choose an *MBTI* personality which best works in that case if a human representative was interacting with the customer. We then collect the opinion of all participants on a drawing board, producing what we call a *personality table.*

Often, participants in a personality workshop disagree about the appropriate *MBTI* for each case and user persona, what could lead to an undesirable outcome of an interface persona with multiple personalities. The facilitator should work on the drawing board to identify the most common personality types, trying to converge to a single, most useful personality type which can handle well most usecases and users. In some cases, it may be necessary to delay the decision process and work with two or more candidate personalities, to be explored further during the rest of the design process before the final choice is made. We also ask each participant to think about someone they know (friend, colleague, etc.) who has that kind of personality, and to use that specific person as a reference in the rest of the design process.

Test Workshop Results

Figure 1 shows a photo of a participant of the first workshop working on his own choice of personalities and the resulting personality table gathering inputs from all participants. In this particular workshop they flocked towards an extroverted personality to handle cases of failed delivery (possible to assertively assure that a new delivery was scheduled) but considered an introverted personality as more effective in the case where the product shipped was incorrect (perhaps to apologize better for what is a basic mistake). In the end, weighing all the cases and customer personas, the group concluded that the most adequate personality would be of *ESFJ* type. In a nutshell, *ESPJ* defines people who are patient, efficient, hard-working, loyal, and, most important, great at following through projects. We then asked all participants to think of a friend

Fig. 1. *Personality workshop*: photo and *personality table* (based on [8]) from the test workshop.

or family member with those characteristics and to imagine (silently) how he or she would handle those usecases.

Our experience doing personality workshops is that they are very good to make participants start seeing the interface as having a human face, and to highlight the importance of coherence in terms of human traits. Having a good initial characterization of the personality of the personified interface helps to ground all the other design methods. In particular, each participant should keep in mind a personal reference of a person of the identified personality, to be used as a touch stone in the subsequent phases of the design process.

4.3 The Conflict Battle Workshop

The second design method we propose explores the behavior a given personality of the interface persona with the user personas in specific scenarios of conflict. We call this method *conflict battle*, because we encourage participants of the design workshop to enact physically conflict scenarios. Several theatrical methods are employed to expose the root causes of the conflict and to amplify it.

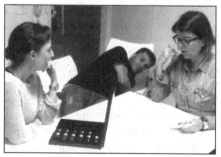

Fig. 2. *Conflict battle:* photo of a *conflict pantomime* and a *conflict observation sheet* from test workshop (extracted from [8]).

The main result of the conflict battle is a series of *conflict pantomimes*, short theatrical skits displaying the social behaviors and emotions involved in actual conflict cases. We use both techniques of *improv* [28] and *pantomime* [29] to encourage theatrical interplay, proposing to the participants the following "rules of engagement":

1. Agree (respect what your partner has created).
2. Not only say "Yes." Say "Yes, and…".
3. Make statements.
4. There are no mistakes… only opportunities.
5. Exaggerate… and then a little more.
6. React only to what happened.
7. Think aloud to the audience.

Rules 1 to 4 are standard in improvisational theatre while rules 5 to 7 aim to externalize emotions, following techniques used in pantomimes. To direct the flow of the conflict pantomimes, the workshop facilitator should employ techniques used by theatre directors such as stopping the action, silencing temporarily one of the players, switching actors, and sometimes proposing specific directions to the development of the action. Every skit should explore thoroughly the complexity of each conflict scenario and the different emotional and cognitive reactions it generates. The participants acting the pantomime should focus in the interplay, not taking notes, committing to memory the skit as a scene which can be re-enacted again during the design process.

Some of the participants who are not part of the skit are told to take photos of the key moments; others are asked take notes on the *conflict observation sheet*, where they record the observed social behaviors (such as aggression, altruism, empathy) and emotions exhibited by the "actors" and the personified machine. We have employed the list of emotions based on Ekman's theory [25] but allow observers to include others as they judge necessary. They also record interpersonal social phenomena such as social influence, group dynamics, pro- and anti-social behaviors, attraction, and self-deception.

After the conflict pantomimes are created and explored, participants focus on ways to mitigate conflicts. Participants should try variations of the conflict scenarios where conflict may be reduced, or its effects diminished. They do so by re-enacting segments of the conflict skits using, for instance, different participants, alternative personalities of the personified interface, and alternative customer personas. For instance, they can try to make the personified machine to be more subservient, shy, or talkative.

Test Workshop Results

In the test workshops, we started by giving participants a sheet of paper with a table containing the *list of usecases* as rows and the *customer personas* as columns and were asked to fill in, from their own personal experiences, typical situations of conflict. Since most of them were familiar with similar e-commerce situations and scenarios, this was easily done.

Before starting the pantomimes, we did some relaxation and warm up theatrical exercises, to address some level of uneasiness we have detected. But in all workshops, participants became eventually very active in creating the improvisational skit. Figure 2 shows a photo of one of the sessions and the corresponding conflict observation sheet, with the observed emotions and social behaviors.

Conflict aroused almost immediately between the participants portraying the customer and the service providers, and often escalated to strong emotions. Many times, the "employees" of the service providers immediately took the side of the provider and start behaving aggressively to customers. For instance, suspicion about the veracity and accuracy of customer reports and justifications was often detected in the back-office, resulting in excuses and false impediments being communicated to the "customers". Like in real life, the participants playing the customers became quickly very upset.

The *conflict pantomimes* were re-enacted two to three times to consolidate them in the participants' memory and allow more detailed observation. We also rotate the participants and observers in the different roles. After each conflict pantomime was consolidated, we asked participants to produce variations where the conflict was better resolved. We employed here some improv techniques such as freezing selectively the action of some participant or rewinding the action to a turning point. For instance, we had a situation where the participants created a pantomime where Melvin, a color-blind customer, was returning a sneaker which he had mistakenly selected, a recurring problem he had with the website. The customer service handler (who did not know about his impairment) was, of course, suspicious about the multiple returns. During one of the re-enactments, one the "employee" participants had the idea to ask the customer if he had any trouble using the website. This gave the customer an opportunity to explain his difficulty with colors and to decrease the "employee's" suspicion of foul play, without having to ask a direct question related to the suspicion which could have offended the "customer".

4.4 The Comics Workshop

It is key for designers to have sketching tools which represent well the design space, allow exploration of that space, and can be used to communicate ideas with stakeholders [30]. We developed a design tool which we call a *comics storyboard,* based on using a hybrid between a *comics story* (more precisely, a *photo novel*) and an interaction storyboard. Beyond the traditional storyboard used in interface design, we include photos of the participants enacting the conflict pantomimes together with typical markings from comics such as balloons to make explicit the inner thoughts and emotions of the user and the personified machine. The comics storyboards are used to explore the personified interface in terms of character consistency, clarity, enjoyment, and quality of conflict resolution.

To facilitate the transition between the conflicting pantomimes and the comics storyboard, participants start by creating an annotated *interaction script* which is a written summary of the main actions of a conflict pantomime and their associated emotions and social behaviors. This script guides the construction of the comics storyboard. After creating the interaction scripts, groups or individuals work separately crafting each frame of the comics storyboard using photos taken during the conflict pantomime. The goal is to obtain a workable, rich representation of key aspects of the interaction, the main conflicts, the human traits at play, and the emotions and social behaviors involved.

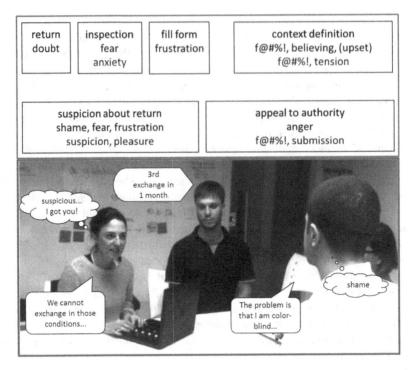

Fig. 3. *Comics workshop*: *interaction script* and *comics storyboard* from the test workshop (extracted from [8]).

Test Workshop Results

In our test workshops the *interaction scripts* were created by the whole group with the help of a whiteboard. Figure 3 shows a transcript from one of the *interaction scripts* created for a *conflict pantomime* for the return scenario involving Melvin discussed before. The first line of each block in the interaction script corresponds to the main action, the second line to the emotions and social behaviors of the customer, and the third line to emotions and social behaviors of the employees.

Figure 3 also shows one frame of the comics storyboard corresponding to the block "suspicion about return" of the interaction script. The frame shows the dialogue exchanges, the emotions and thoughts of the participants during the pantomimes (inside "mental" balloons), including the ones from "the system", the customer database which tracks the customers, which was also enacted by a participant (see the balloon with the text "3rd exchange in 1 month" of Fig. 3).

We found that the production of the *interaction scripts*, was essential to make the production of the *comics storyboard* easier, since it gathered the basic structure of the pantomime and its main components. The overall result was a very concise and rich representation of the key aspects and the conflicts of the self-service process.

4.5   The Puppet Prototyping Workshop

After working out the range of human exchanges, emotions, and social behaviors to be performed by the personified interface, using *conflict battles,* and registering them as *comics storyboards*, the next step is to transform the comics storyboards into concrete interface actions which can express the correct social behaviors and emotions. We call this *puppet prototyping*, a workshop where participants examine the conflict pantomimes they have developed and transform dialogue and human actions into appropriate interface actions, using some of the techniques such as the *Stanislavsky's system* and the concepts and processes from puppetry and movie animation discussed before.

Participants are first asked to create *action pantomimes*, a version of the conflict pantomimes where emotions and social behaviors are expressed through interface actions and not verbally. A useful technique is to re-enact the conflict pantomimes using *constricted dialoguing techniques*. For example, participants may be restricted to use very short sentences, or only gestures, or not facing each other, or pretending to be animals. By exploring the limits of human expression, it is possible to find mechanisms which convey non-verbally the social behaviors and emotions of the conflict pantomimes. The actions are recorded into the comics storyboard, replacing or augmenting the original dialogue.

We then ask the participants to create the *interface comics*, a sequence of interface actions associated with each of the frames of the comics storyboard. We do so by having participants re-enact the action pantomimes not using any dialogue or physical actions but resorting solely to interface actions which are afforded by the actual computer interface, drawn on sheets of paper. The sheets of paper are then lined on the wall and improved until ready to be incorporated as a line at the bottom of the corresponding on the comics storyboard. Participants can then critique the interface actions considering the juxtaposed human actions, emotions, and social behaviors they should be expressing. They can then iteratively explore and refine further the interface comics doing more exploratory work with constricted dialoguing or by considering alternative interface actions.

By iteratively rewriting the interface comics and looking at it as the narrative constructed with the user, at the end of the puppet prototyping workshop a complete interface storyboard is produced to guide the actual implementation of the interface. Notice that the interface comics is more expressive than traditional storyboards since it documents the emotions, actions, emotions, and social behaviors of the users and of the personified interface.

Fig. 4. *Puppet prototyping workshop*: photos (extracted from [8]), modified *comic storyboard* and *interface comics* from the test workshop.

Test Workshop Results

Participants of the test workshops were surprised and even initially reluctant to explore constricted dialogue techniques. For many, it seemed straightforward to create interface storyboards from the *comics storyboards*. Figure 4 shows a photo taken during one of the re-enactments of a *conflict pantomime* where participants were not allowed to use words. During that exercise, participants discovered that they could convey the concern of the employee about the repeated return of products by showing the customer the information about the three consecutive returns in just one month, without explicitly stating suspicion.

This finding was represented into the comics storyboard, as shown in Fig. 4, by hashing the recorded exchange to indicate its substitution by a display action where the three previous product exchanges are shown to the customer. The depiction of this new way to handle the situation in the *comics storyboard* makes it clear that the intention of the action is to communicate suspicion in a "polite" form and not be informative to the customer.

In our test workshops we saw sometimes participants forgetting some of the findings from the *conflict battle* phase. We found one of the key functions of the *comics storyboard* is to keep the search for interface solutions focused on addressing the key conflicts and the appropriate handling of the customer's emotions.

5   Discussion

There is a growing demand and opportunity for personified interfaces. In this paper we explored key aspects involved in their design. First, we listed three key, new requirements which are specific to personified interfaces: coherent human traits, dealing with conflict, and handling drama, as initially discussed in [8]. Following, we presented four design methods inspired by previous work on service design [7], adapting theories and techniques from social psychology, personality theory, emotion theory, acting, puppetry, movie animation.

The four design methods are aimed to work the design of the personified interface towards to: a better definition of the human personality to be perceived by the user (*personality workshop*); unearthing and mitigating the main conflicts and associated emotions to be handled by the interface (*conflict battles*); creating a rich representation of the dramatized interaction and using it to explore the space of design solutions (*comics storyboard*); and transforming into interface actions the solutions found through theatrical methods (*puppet prototyping*).

Those four design methods were tested in three design workshops conducted to design a service recovery interface for a hypothetical shoe e-commerce website. Examples from the workshop were described in some detail, in particular, the case of handling the complaint of a visually impaired customer whose behavior aroused suspicion. We showed in this example how the four methods, working together, contributed to find an original solution which minimized conflict and handled properly many of the emotions related to the process.

After the test workshops we conducted informal debriefs of the participants. Many of them commented on how they were surprised on how naturally the design methods revealed the emotions and conflicts and led the participants to find ways to mitigate them. *"They were very effective on cutting the [expletive deleted] and make us talk about what was actually happening"* said one of the participants. In terms of difficulties, there were some initial uneasiness with the theatrical techniques, especially he more unusual ones during the puppet prototyping part. In the first workshop we had more time to make the participants relax and do a couple of theatrical warming up games, and that seemed to have helped.

Of course, there are many unanswered questions regarding the proposed design methods. We are looking forward to applying those the methods to real cases of personified interface design, especially in the context of designing chatbots and personal assistants, and so be able to evaluate much better how effective they are in practice. There is certainly still much to be learned about the design of personified interfaces. But we hope ideas in this paper, although still in formation and not thoroughly tested, can be an initial a guide for designers facing the challenge of creating interfaces which convey human traits and behaviors.

Acknowledgements. We thank the participants of the workshops who gracefully agreed to allow the use in this paper of the photos and other materials produced during the workshops. We thank Heloisa Candello for references and discussions about designing chatbots.

References

1. Reeves, B., Nass, C.: The Media Equation: How People Treat Computers, Television, and New Media like Real People and Places. CSLI, Stanford (1996)
2. Luger, E., Sellen, A.: Like having a really bad PA. In: Proceedings of the 2016 CHI Conference on Human Factors in Computing Systems - CHI 2016, pp. 5286–5297. ACM Press, New York (2016)
3. Nass, C.I., Brave, S.: Wired for Speech: How Voice Activates and Advances the Human-Computer Relationship. MIT Press, Cambridge (2005)
4. Shevat, A.: Designing Bots: Creating Conversational Experiences. O'Reilly Media, Sebastopol (2017)
5. Pearl, C.: Designing Voice User Interfaces: Principles of Conversational Experiences. O'Reilly Media, Sebastopol (2016)
6. Laurel, B.: Computers as Theatre. Addison-Wesley, Reading (1991)
7. Pinhanez, C.S.: Borg-human interaction design. In: Proceedings of the Fourth Service Design and Service Innovation Conference (ServDes 2014), Lancaster, England, pp. 100–109 (2014)
8. Pinhanez, C.S.: Design methods for personified interfaces. In: Proceedings of the 1st International Conference on Computer-Human Interaction Research and Applications. INSTICC, Funchal (2017)
9. Tajfel, H.: Human Groups and Social Categories. Studies in Social Psychology. Cambridge University Press, Cambridge, England (1981)
10. Lee, E.J., Nass, C., Brave, S.: Can computer-generated speech have gender? In: CHI 2000 Extended Abstracts on Human Factors in Computing Systems - CHI 2000, pp. 289–290 (2000)
11. Nass, C., Takayama, L., Brave, S.: Socializing consistency. In: Zhang, P., Galletta, D.F. (eds.) Human-Computer Interaction and Management Information Systems, pp. 373–392. ME Sharpe (2006)
12. Nass, C., Najmi, S.: Race vs. culture in computer-based agents and users: implications for internationalizing websites (2002)
13. Li, J., Ju, W., Reeves, B.: Touching a mechanical body: tactile contact with intimate parts of a human-shaped robot is physiologically arousing. In: Proceedings of the 66th Annual International Communication Association Conference. ICA, Fukuoka (2016)
14. Breazeal, C.: Emotion and sociable humanoid robots. Int. J. Hum. Comput. Stud. **59**, 119–155 (2003). https://doi.org/10.1016/S1071-5819(03)00018-1
15. Dennett, D.C.: Intentional systems. In: Haugeland, J. (ed.) Mind Design: Philosophy, Psychology, Artificial Intelligence. MIT Press, Cambridge (1981)
16. Newman, M.L., Groom, C.J., Handelman, L.D., Pennebaker, J.W.: Gender differences in language use: an analysis of 14,000 text samples. Discourse Process. **45**, 211–236 (2008). https://doi.org/10.1080/01638530802073712
17. Lee, E.-J.: Effects of "gender" of the computer on informational social influence: the moderating role of task type. Int. J. Hum. Comput. Stud. **58**, 347–362 (2003). https://doi.org/10.1016/S1071-5819(03)00009-0
18. Giles, H., Scherer, K.R.: Social Markers in Speech. Cambridge University Press, Cambridge, England (1979)
19. Tajfel, H.: Social identity and intergroup behaviour. Soc. Sci. Inf. **13**, 65–93 (1974). https://doi.org/10.1177/053901847401300204

20. Nass, C., Lee, K.M.: Does computer-synthesized speech manifest personality? Experimental tests of recognition, similarity-attraction, and consistency-attraction. J. Exp. Psychol. Appl. **7**, 171–181 (2001). https://doi.org/10.1037//1076-898X.7.3.171
21. Stanislavsky, C.: Building a Character. Routledge/Theater Arts Books, New York (1949)
22. Blumenthal, E.: Puppetry: A World History. Harry N. Abrams Publishers, New York (2005)
23. Thomas, F., Johnston, O.: Disney Animation: The Illusion of Life. Abbeville Press, New York (1981)
24. Myers, I.B.: MBTI Manual: A Guide to the Development and Use of the Myers-Briggs Type Indicator. Consulting Psychologists Press, Palo Alto (1998)
25. Ekman, P., Friesen, W.V.: Unmasking the Face: A Guide to Recognizing Emotions from Facial Clues. Prentice-Hall, Englewood Cliffs (1975)
26. Plutchik, R.: Emotion: A Psychoevolutionary Synthesis. HarperCollins College Division, New York (1980)
27. Pruitt, J., Adlin, T.: The Persona Lifecycle: Keeping People in Mind Throughout Product Design. Morgan Kaufmann Publishers, Boston (2006)
28. Johnstone, K.: IMPRO: Improvisation and Theatre. Methuen Drama, England (1981)
29. Barba, E., Savarese, N.: Dictionary of Theatre Anthropology: The Secret Art of the Performer. Routledge, London, England (1991)
30. Buxton, W.: Sketching User Experience: Getting the Design Right and the Right Design. Morgan Kaufmann, San Francisco (2007)

Improving Operator Situation Awareness Through Ecological Interfaces: Lessons from Aviation

Max Mulder[✉], Clark Borst, and Marinus M. van Paassen

Faculty of Aerospace Engineering, TU Delft, Delft, The Netherlands
{m.mulder,c.borst,m.m.vanpaassen}@tudelft.nl

Abstract. The purpose of human-machine systems design is to develop interfaces and automation tools which support human operators in performing effective, efficient and safe work. An important prerequisite for the latter is that operators understand the process under control, are aware of what is happening, and have sufficient means to act on the process appropriately. In this chapter, which is an extension of our CHIRA'2017 paper [1], we discuss the ecological approach we adopted to design human-machine systems in aviation. We focus in particular on what, in our opinion, operator situation awareness actually means, and how to improve it. The aircraft separation task will be discussed, using two examples which show how novel visualizations and tools can support pilots and air traffic controllers in their decision making.

Keywords: Human-machine systems · Aviation · Automation · Situation awareness · Ecological interface design · Cockpits · Air traffic control

1 Introduction

In today's highly-automated cockpits, computers perform the majority of the work, and pilots are responsible for monitoring and supervising the automation functions and performance. In the vast majority of cases this leads to a satisfactory performance, but in cases where automation fails, the crew can sometimes be confronted with situations where they must make split-second decisions on how to proceed, causing peak levels of workload, and sometimes putting the aircraft and its passengers in dangerous situations.

Root causes for incidents and accidents can be that, because of casual slips in maintenance or extremely bad weather conditions, basic sensors to measure for instance an aircraft velocity and height fail. These failures can propagate through the automated functions, causing automation to function improperly, or stop working altogether. Tragic examples are Air France flight 447 (which crashed into the Atlantic Ocean on May 31, 2009, killing all crew and passengers) and Turkish Airlines flight 1951 (which crashed near Amsterdam Airport Schiphol on February 27, 2009, with nine fatal casualties).

© Springer Nature Switzerland AG 2019
A. Holzinger et al. (Eds.): CHIRA 2017, CCIS 654, pp. 20–44, 2019.
https://doi.org/10.1007/978-3-030-32965-5_2

Many argue that, because of the persistent human contribution to causing mishaps one should strive for eliminating the human pilots from the cockpit. Clearly, in the past decades our automation systems have become smarter and more versatile agents, and will continue to do so in the decades to come, with the steep advent of artificial intelligence (AI) techniques. The current state-of-the-art in the latter shows, however, that although progress in 'weak AI' is indeed very steep, with computer minds beating human minds in every possible game, and even several pattern recognition tasks where humans used to be far superior, advances in 'deep AI' are much, much slower. And it is in fact the latter intelligence that we need when replacing pilots, namely intelligence that can 'think about' and deal with (ideally, all possible) situations – complex, lumped and nested combinations of events, states – based on incomplete and uncertain, noisy information. It is safe to say that, since the omniscient HAL 9000 computer featured in Stanley Kubrick's classical science fiction movie "2001 A Space Odyssey" (1968, fifty years ago) is not quite there yet, human pilots will remain to be the *only intelligent agent on-board* that is capable of dealing with unanticipated events. Since these unexpected variations are abundant and bound to happen in open systems like aircraft, we expect that pilots will remain to be the main safety net, our last line of defense, in aviation for a long time.

Given the fact that we will continue to have human pilots working in cockpits for the foreseeable future, the work in our lab focuses on supporting them in their work, through developing better training programs, better interfaces, and clever automation tools. From the examples above it is clear that, in situations where sensors, automation – basically *anything* that can go wrong both inside and outside the aircraft that has an effect on safe flight – do not function properly, it is crucial that pilots have, or quickly regain, a good awareness and understanding of the situation at hand. Hence, *situation awareness* (SA) is key, and it is no surprise that this term pops up in many, if not all, studies on human-machine interfaces in aviation and beyond since the late 1980s.

In this book chapter[1] we therefore start in Sect. 2 with a discussion on *situation awareness* (SA), its many definitions, and our take on what it actually means to be 'aware' of 'situations'. We then briefly touch upon how the modern flight deck evolved from the classical cockpit, and the lessons we can learn from that, in Sect. 3. The 'ecological approach' to interface design, as proposed by Vicente and Rasmussen in the early 1990s, [2,3], has been adopted in our lab, and will be discussed in Sect. 4. We recently published an extensive review of our work, see [4].

We then discuss two examples of our approach to designing interfaces in aviation. In the extensive first example, Sect. 5, we describe the process of how we designed an ecological interface to support pilots in performing the (future)

---

[1] This chapter is an extended version of our conference paper presented as a keynote speaker's contribution to the first *International Conference on Computer-Human Interaction Research and Applications* conference held in Madeira (CHIRA 2017), [1]. Extensive parts of this paper have been copied, but we re-organized it and also added one more example to explain our approach.

task of self-separation. Here, pilots must change their aircraft state (heading, speed, altitude) in such a way that they do not interfere with the trajectories of other aircraft surrounding them. The new interface attempts to capture and visualize the separation 'situation' in such a way that pilots can directly see what the situation "is", what it "means" and "if and how to respond to it", all in the context of being responsible for a safe and productive flight.

The second example, Sect. 6, will then briefly discuss how the 'lessons learned' from the design of an airborne self-separation display were used to develop a similar interface to support air traffic controllers, who are currently doing this separation task from the ground.

The chapter will end with some closing statements in Sect. 7.

2   Situation Awareness

Since the rapid increase of automation levels in the cockpit in the mid 1980s, situation awareness studies have dominated research and development of current and novel human-machine systems in aviation. Pioneering work was conducted by Endsley, leading to her three-level model comprising 'perception', 'comprehension' and 'projection' [5,6] and the following definition of SA: *"the perception of environmental elements and events with respect to time or space, the comprehension of their meaning, and the projection of their status into the future"*. The concept of situation awareness has been the subject of many follow-up studies and often heated scientific debates on whether it is properly grounded in theory. Literature surveys showed that quickly after its first inception already more than twenty-seven other possible 'definitions' of the SA concept were published [7].

Despite the ongoing debate on proper definitions and grounding of situation awareness in cognitive science, the concept is very often used in evaluating the quality of human-machine interfaces. It is assumed that a 'good' interface leads to a 'high level' of SA, and vice versa. Then, to 'measure' SA, a variety of tools has been developed over the years that allow experimenters to include SA as one of the dependent measures (besides mental workload, human-machine system performance, etc.) in their evaluations. Examples are SPAM, SAGAT, SABARS, WOMBAT, SART, etcetera, that all aim to measure the 'awareness' of the operator; again, see [7] for an overview.

Typical for most studies, is that experimenters determine beforehand *what* the operator *should be aware of* in a particular task, and then measure the level in which this is indeed the case, or not. An example is whether pilots know the aircraft velocity and height above terrain during an approach to landing, which are indeed crucial for safety and performance. A too low velocity may cause the aircraft to stall, a too high velocity may cause it to hit the runway surface too hard. But apart from these clear-cut cases that are easily understood, and the awareness of which can be measured without much difficulty, the analysis of "what needs to be known" by pilots becomes more cumbersome (and also more challenging to measure) when the situation becomes more complicated. It is a fact that measuring the operator's awareness of certain system 'states' does not mean that the operator truly and fully *understands* what exactly is happening, which may require a deeper understanding of the functioning of the system, and the various means available to reach the ends of operating safely and effectively.

As an example, again consider the situation where an aircraft is making an approach to landing, using a conventional three-degree glide path as a reference. When the aircraft is, at some point during the approach, flying higher than the reference path with a velocity that is somewhat too low, then surely we can measure the 'awareness' of the pilot of the fact that these two states are off-nominal, by asking her about her altitude and speed relative to the path. However, we do *not* measure the awareness of the pilot that in this *situation* she can bring both states back to their nominal values by simply *exchanging* the higher-than-required potential energy (height) with the lower-than-required kinetic energy (speed), through using the elevator control to put the nose of the aircraft down. We argue that the responsibility for understanding this situation lies not only in the pilot, but also in the experimenter, who should ask the 'right' question about what this situation actually means, and analyze the different representations in which one can frame the questions on SA.

In the work in our lab we therefore aim to obtain knowledge about what 'situations' actually are. That is, whereas many in the human factors community focus on studying the 'awareness' part of operators when dealing with situations which the experimenter has (hopefully) analyzed in full detail, to ask the operator the 'right' questions to measure SA, we put most of our efforts in understanding the situations [8]. In other words, rather than looking 'inside' the operator's head to see what she is aware of, we first focus on the environment 'outside' the operator, to analyze what she should be aware of when pursuing a particular goal.

In this chapter we will briefly discuss our approach, which is based on an analysis of the work domain at various levels of abstraction, adopting the key elements and tools of Rasmussen's and Vicente's 'ecological' approach to interface design [2,3,9]. But before we start with discussing the ecological approach, let's first take a look at how flight deck instruments and automation developed in the past decades.

3   Flight Deck Design

Figure 1 illustrates how, in the past 50 years, the classic aircraft cockpit – comprised of many individual electro-mechanical instruments – evolved to become the modern "glass cockpit" – with large electronic and programmable displays. Introducing novel automation has reduced the flight crew to only two persons, and changed the role of the pilot from a manual controller to a supervisor of a highly-automated, complex system [10,11].

In the 1960s' cockpits of commercial aircraft, all available information was presented to the pilots, navigators and flight deck engineer on a large array of electro-mechanical instruments. Generally speaking, everything that could be measured was presented, in an attempt to provide the humans on-board

(a) classic

(b) modern

Fig. 1. Evolution of the aviation flight deck.

with as much information as possible. The crew then had to integrate all this information, and form a "mental picture" of the current state of the aircraft, predict that state and act on it in a way that satisfied the mission goals. Most of the "cognition" was to be done by the human operators and because of the plethora of information and the dial-and-gauge interface design, their workload was (in some phases of flight, such as landing) very high, leading to low task performance. Human errors were everywhere. This led cockpit design engineers to conclude that, apparently, despite all their efforts in creating cockpits that contained all information necessary to fly, the task is in fact too difficult for humans and could perhaps be done better by computers.

Hence, in the modern cockpit most of the basic flying tasks (closing the nested loops of control, guidance, and navigation) have been automated, and most of the work to be done *and the corresponding cognition needed* to perform the job was moved to clever computer algorithms. As a result, most of the time the workload is low, to (steeply) increase only in situations that are unanticipated by the automation designers, causing the automation to malfunction or not function at all. And here it is where the other side of the automation coin appears. Driven away from the basic control loops, the pilots sometimes have low situation awareness, must make split-second decisions in situations that automation cannot handle, potentially contributing to human error.

In the evolution from the classic cockpit to the modern flight deck, several useful and important interface design principles have been developed. Examples are studies that stress the importance of proper illumination, readability, and the use of colors and symbols, and later studies that have led to the 'laws' of integrated, configural or object displays, emergent features and the "principle of the moving part" [12,13]. These design principles are valid and improve access to data, the transfer of information from sensors to humans. They provide little help, however, for the designer to determine the "right" representation of the world, one that facilitates human-automation teamwork, and supports the human pilot's creative abilities.

Classic cockpits are examples of a design philosophy called a "single sensor, single indicator" (SSSI) [2], where one presents all information available in a readable format, communicating with the humans on the level of *signals* [14]. Since it is very difficult for pilots to integrate all this information, automation was introduced to help them improve their performance and reduce their workload, moving much of the thinking to be done into computer algorithms. Within their limited scope of the problem domain, these algorithms perform automatically, sometimes warning the pilots for potential 'problems', i.e., communicating with them on the level of *signs*, intended to elicit predetermined (trained) solutions to situations that were anticipated in the design of the automation. But what about situations that were not anticipated beforehand, that extend beyond the limited scope of the algorithms? How to deal with the inevitable unanticipated variability in this complex domain?

We believe that, in the absence of some omniscient artificially intelligent entity that can cope with this variability, we should strive for supporting productive thinking of pilots, enabling them to creatively invent solutions to these emergent, unexpected, multi-dimensional problems. This requires that pilots learn and maintain representations of the deep structure of the work domain, through proper training and working with interfaces that communicate *situations*.

4   Ecological Approach

In our work, we strive for a human-machine system – defined here as automation and interfaces – that *shares* the cognitive work between the automation and humans. It is clear that much of the work to be done can be performed much better (more accurate, much faster, with many dimensions to simultaneously optimize) by computer algorithms. But since these algorithms are invariably – and perhaps even inevitably – limited in their scope and understanding of the world in which they operate, at some point the crew needs to be involved to decide in situations where automation cannot decide, or interfere in situations where automation fails. We aim for a work environment where the crew is involved, with reasonable workload, high SA, working on representations of the world that can be *shared* between automated and human agents [15–17].

One of the main starting points of our work is the classification that a flight deck as an *open* system [9]. It has many "interfaces" with its environment, e.g., weather, other traffic, terrain, air traffic control (ATC). It has an extensive and sometimes rather complicated interaction with the environment, which makes its operation to be unpredictable, and *one cannot imagine and anticipate for all possible events in advance.* In the absence of an infinitely clever computer agent, as we see in science fiction movies (e.g., HAL9000), we continue to depend on the intelligence and adaptability of humans to deal with the unanticipated variability, the known and unknown unknowns.

To support humans in their cognitive work, it is important to consider one of the main strengths of the human mind. One of the distinctive features of human intelligence is our amazing capacity to learn, detect and use patterns and relations between our actions and what we perceive. Hence, we attempt to design graphical representations that provide 'natural' patterns that are linked to functionally-relevant relations among the state variables, such that humans become 'aware' of situations with minimal cognitive effort. Our interface designs literally "show" the problem space to the pilot, and allow her to "work" on it, in such a way that she can use the display representation as a template. This "problem space," however, is often not normally visible to the human eye, as in our everyday activities such as grasping a cup of coffee, walk through a shopping center, and ride a bicycle in busy traffic.

In his "ecological" approach to visual perception, Gibson emphasizes the "direct perception" capabilities of humans, and the direct couplings that exist between perception and action [18,19]. He introduced the concept of "affordance", possibilities and constraints for actions and achieving goals, specified by the natural environment. Take for example a pile of wood found on a beach. Depending on the situation at hand, a cold person could make a fire to warm-up, a hungry person would use the fire to prepare food; Robinson Crusoe would perhaps try to make a raft; when it starts raining one could try to create an opportunity for shelter. This is just a sub-set of possible meanings that the pile of wood may have for an actor in the environment, all specified by the natural display that can be directly perceived.

Vicente and Rasmussen took this stance when proposing their "ecological approach" to design interfaces for complex systems [2,3]. In Ecological Interface Design (EID) one aims to transfer the cognitive process of understanding and interacting with complex systems to a *perceptual* process, where operators interact with representations of that complex process on (usually graphical) interfaces. An important difference with interacting in the natural world is that complex systems do often not allow humans to "step-in and explore". Rather, the interface is the *medium* for interaction, and an ecological interface should try to reveal the deep structure of the work domain in a way that is compatible with human perception, to *make visible the invisible.*

In his book "Cognitive Work Analysis," Vicente proposes six steps in the development of an ecological display: Work Domain Analysis, Control Task Analysis, Strategies Analysis, an Analysis of Social Organization and Cooperation, Worker Competencies Analysis, and finally the interface design [9]. The Work Domain Analysis (WDA) is the most important one, as here the interface designer must analyze the basic functioning of the work domain for which the system has to fulfil its purpose. Rather than trying to understand the cognitive processes that may guide the operator (or computer algorithm) in doing the work, the WDA focuses on the environment and the ways in which the world constraints and physical laws afford actions. Developing an appropriate representation of this "action space," *independent of the human or automated agent* – a representation that is true and valid for both – stands at the center of the ecological approach.

In the past decades we developed several ecological interfaces for the flight deck. Examples are a Total Energy management display for basic aircraft symmetrical flight control, that enables pilots to understand and act on exchanging their aircraft potential and kinetic energy [20], Separation Assistance displays that allow pilots to better understand and act on other traffic [21–24], an ecological Synthetic Vision display [25–27], and a display to manipulate four-dimensional (position and time) aircraft trajectories [28, 29] We also explored various EID designs for air traffic controllers in current and future air traffic management environments [16, 17, 30–33], and controllers of multiple unmanned aerial vehicles [34]. We will discuss two examples of our work in the next sections, focusing on the aircraft separation task performed by pilots in the cockpit, or by air traffic controllers on the ground.

5   First Example: Airborne Self-separation

In the first example we discuss the development of an ecological interface that was designed to support pilots in the future task of maintaining a safe separation with other traffic flying in the vicinity of their own aircraft. Currently this is a task done by air traffic control, but in the future parts of the airspace may become unmanaged, and here the pilots and their automation systems will become responsible for the separation task [35].

An airborne separation assistance system (ASAS) involves *"the equipment, protocols, airborne surveillance and <...> which enable the pilot to exercise responsibility, <...> for separation of his aircraft from one or more aircraft"* (ICAO SICASP/6-WP/44). The ASAS functionalities, i.e., the work to be done by automation and/or pilot, include: (i) maintaining an overview of the surrounding traffic; (ii) detecting potential loss of separation conflicts; (iii) resolving conflicts and (iv) preventing aircraft from running into new conflicts. Note that a 'conflict' is defined here as a *potential* loss of separation, in the future.

The development of ASAS systems has received a lot of attention in the past decades and various prototypes have been built and tested (for an overview see [36]). Common to many ASAS designs is that they rely on trajectory prediction algorithms which compute the "closest point of approach" (CPA) between the own aircraft and another aircraft, and then have another computer algo-rithm "reason about" the best way to deal with situations where the CPA is predicted to become too small. Typically these algorithms are programmed into a computer, and then the interface designer is brought into play to create the interface. In the light of the discussion in Sect. 3: all cognition is being put into the computer, hidden from the pilot, and communication is done at the level of signals (where is the other aircraft?) and signs (are we moving too close? warn the pilot!).

Not surprisingly, in many ASAS evaluations the typical 'ironies' of automa-tion [37,38] appeared: hidden rationale, confusion of the automation intent, dis-agreement, lack of trust or complacency, low situation awareness. "Why does the automation propose this solution?", "What will happen when I follow the automation's advice?", and "What if I don't?".

Apart from these issues, it is a fact that there will always be cases which the automation designers and engineers did not think of, because of the open and complex nature of interaction of the aircraft in its environment. Automation is human, by design, possibly including human mistakes as well, but of a different kind; it is limited in its rationale by design, through what it is programmed to do. In addition, cockpit automation is typically only aware of a *part* of the situation (e.g., it considers traffic) and ignorant of other constraints to flight (e.g., terrain). Current automation does not fully support pilots in these multi-constraint situations.

Before we start with the WDA, one should keep in mind that self-separation problems typically evolve very slowly. ASAS systems work with time horizons of 3 to 5 min, with aircraft flying several hundreds of miles apart, requiring pilots to zoom out on their navigation display to see the other aircraft, moving very slowly on the display. This makes it very difficult for them to detect possible conflict situations, and manage their resolution. Clearly, there is a need here to make the separation task more "compatible" to human perception, and make visible the invisible.

5.1   Work Domain Analysis

In our work on the ASAS problem, which took us several years, we were inter-ested in finding a different representation of the traffic separation problem, other than the CPA-based solutions developed before. Would there be a way to com-municate with the pilot at the "symbol" level, such that she would understand the separation situation at a glance, directly act on it, with or without the help of automation?

We applied Rasmussen's AH [39], at the five common levels of abstraction: Functional purpose, Abstract function, Generalized function, Physical function and Physical form. Figure 2 illustrates one of the AH's resulting from the anal-ysis. In an effort to construct this abstraction hierarchy, we first started with numerous computer simulations of approaching aircraft, trying to figure out what are the physical laws and abstract functions that govern the dynamics of the separation control problem. At each particular level, one considers the work

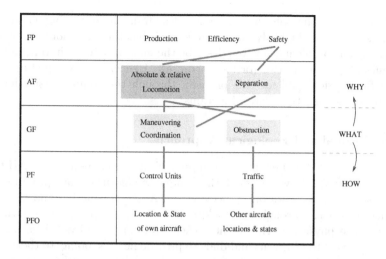

Fig. 2. Abstraction Hierarchy for the separation assistance work domain.

domain at that level of abstraction, answering the question "WHAT" happens on this level? Going one level up then answers the question of "WHY" we have this function, and moving one level down then answers "HOW" the function is being performed.

An analysis of computer simulations of aircraft flying in a two-dimensional airspace led us to the insight that two "travel functions" form the core of the separation problem. These act at the Abstract function level of the AH: 'absolute and relative locomotion', and 'separation' [21]. Manipulating the relative motion of aircraft requires aircraft to maneuver, and these maneuvers should be coordinated such that separation is maintained; these are the Generalized functions.

At the highest level, Functional purpose, the goal of having an ASAS system is defined: ensure safety at all times. This was obvious from the start, but our simulations led us to add two more: be productive and efficient. For particular geometries we discovered that some maneuvers were indeed safe, but would lead to situations where aircraft needed to make a more than 90° turn, or even fly back, or that it would take very long for the conflict to be resolved.

Figure 2 shows that at the Physical function level we see the actual traffic that flies within the vicinity of the own aircraft, and the control units that pilots have to manipulate the generalized functions: their cockpit interfaces to autopilot, throttle and flight management systems. At the Physical form level we see the state of the own aircraft and the locations and states of the other aircraft involved.

This AH has had numerous iterations, as can be seen in our publications over the years [21–23]. Indeed, we have been struggling with it for quite some time as, other than in process control where the abstract and generalized functions can be quickly connected to the physics of the plant being controlled [9], in this separation problem the "physics" were not clear from the beginning. Of course, the physics of aircraft flight dynamics are known, but these are not very helpful in this particular problem; they well describe the motions of one aircraft, but not the physics of separating two (or more) aircraft. Hence, we developed our own "meaningful physics" [40] for this problem through the computer simulations stated above, yielding the "travel functions."

5.2 Traditional and Ecological Approach

Reflecting on the "typical engineering approach" in the context of the AH that results from the WDA, we see that the computer algorithms are programmed to "understand" and "work on" especially the Abstract function and Generalized function levels. Through the cockpit interfaces, the pilots are shown the elements of the physical environment (other aircraft), the Physical form level, they have their control buttons and dials to provide new set-points to their automated agents, the Physical function level, and they are trained to understand the signals and signs that the ASAS system provides them at the Functional Purpose level. In this design, pilots will understand *why* the system is there (functional purpose), they are trained *how* to work with the system (physical function, physical form), but they get little insight into how the system actually works and deals with the environmental constraints (abstract and generalized function levels).

In other words, the rationale behind the signals and signs is "hidden" in the automation, and its opaqueness prevents most pilots to obtain a full understanding of how the computer has interpreted and dealt with the traffic situation at the Abstract and Generalized function levels. And indeed this is typical for many of the human-machine systems and automated tools that have been developed for the flight deck, hiding the rationale from the pilots, putting the real cognition and processing of data and situations into actions and advice in pieces of automation that are non-transparent, leading to low situation awareness, workload peaks, and all the ironies of automation.

Clearly then, in an ecological interface design approach the rationale of the automated algorithms and the invisible but crucial elements of the world domain should be visualized. In our designs we therefore aim at "making visible the invisible", showing pilots the "world behind the glass" [41] at the abstract and generalized function levels, such that with or without automated help they can reason about the traffic situation themselves. Without automation they should be able to detect and resolve conflicts themselves and also to do it in a way that is safe, efficient and productive. With automation in place pilots should be able to (much) better understand the signals and signs (warnings and resolution advisories) that the automation provides, as the communication will also show the deep structure that provides a context for interpreting the meaning of these signals and signs as situations [8].

5.3 Traditional Design

In the past 25 years much research has been conducted on the self-separation problem, for instance in the context of the "Free Flight" programs that ran in the 1990s. Numerous attempts were done to support pilots in understanding the essence of traffic conflicts and how the automation deals with them. Early visualizations showed the point of closest approach (CPA) on the navigation display, often graphically put onto the display as ellipsoidal "no-go" zones.

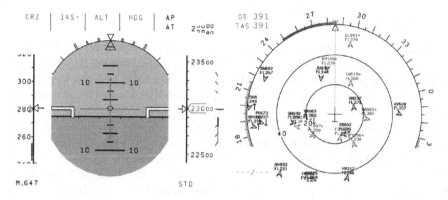

Fig. 3. Predictive ASAS, an earlier design for airborne assistance. On the Primary Flight Display (left): speed bands and vertical speed bands; on the Navigation Display (right): heading bands. Figure obtained from [42].

Evaluations with these no-go zones showed that new conflicts were triggered by maneuvers initiated to resolve other conflicts. Engineers then came up with predictive ASAS, based on computing "heading bands" and "speed bands", which show all possible headings of the own aircraft that would result in a conflict (*assuming constant current speed*) and all possible speeds that would result in a conflict (*assuming constant current heading*), respectively. Figure 3 illustrates how the traditional Primary Flight Display (left) and Navigation Display (right) were extended with the speed bands and heading bands overlays. Here, the own aircraft is safe from conflicts, but the pilot must not initiate any heading changes to the left that are smaller than 35° (heading band), or fly 15 knots slower (speed band).

Later a computer-aided "optimal" solution was also shown, usually a *combination* of speed and heading change, that was the best and most efficient way out of the conflict [36]. With the speed and heading bands, and the optimal solution presented, pilots indeed can see how to avoid other aircraft. They have a hard time, however, finding out themselves what would be the most efficient way to resolve the conflict and especially to see and check whether the computer-aided solution and heading and speed bands are in fact correct. And the optimal solution often appears right into the heading and speed bands that act as "no go" states, as it consists of a combination of heading and speed changes that are smaller than resolving the conflict with either heading or speed. This causes confusion and a lack of confidence, an automation irony at work. In addition, when the own aircraft is involved in a multi-aircraft conflict, more and more no-go bands are presented and it becomes difficult for pilots to relate these to the individual aircraft involved. This iteration of typical engineering and interface design did not end up with an easy-to-use interface. The representation of the problem taken – CPA, heading and speed bands – has in fact obscured the way the world works.

5.4   Ecological Design

We took a different approach to the problem, based on visualizing the full affordances of relative and absolute motion. For a comprehensive description of the design and the process we have gone through, the reader is referred to [21].

When the locations and velocities of all aircraft flying near the own aircraft are known – a safe assumption in current-day aviation – we can compute the set of relative velocity vectors that will bring the own aircraft into a conflict situation with each other aircraft. The pilot must change the velocity *vector* of her own aircraft – its direction (=heading of the own aircraft, the direction in which it flies) and/or magnitude (=speed of the own aircraft, the distance it covers per time unit) – in such a way that its tip does not belong to this set. In this way we developed an own aircraft-centered presentation of this relative motion, which shows the affordances of "hit" and "avoid" that can be directly perceived and acted upon by the pilot (or automation). We later found out that in robotics similar solutions were developed [43–45], after Degré and Lefèvre published a very similar solution in 1981 [46]; we also found the Battenberg course indicator (dating back to 1892) which visualizes ship maneuvering constraints in a similar way. We extended and unified all existing solutions to their full *2D + time* potential in [47].

Figure 4(a) shows the ecological ASAS display, in its most elementary form: a two-dimensional semicircular presentation used as an overlay on the current Navigation Display, Fig. 3 (righ-hand display). Later we also developed vertical [48], co-planar [23,24] and 3-D orthogonal [22] presentations.

Figure 4(b) shows the display elements. The own aircraft 'velocity vector' is the first key element. The size of the vector can be changed, indicating speed changes: it can be made larger (fly faster) or smaller (fly slower), but the length cannot exceed the velocity limits indicated by the two semi-circles. The tip of the velocity vector cannot move out of these limits, which represent constraints "internal" to the *own* aircraft; they depend on performance limits (physical function level in the abstraction hierarchy). The direction of the vector can also change, i.e., rotated to the left and right, indicating heading changes. Heading changes larger than 90° left or right are possible but are considered to be not very productive (functional purpose in the AH).

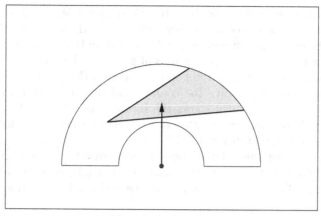

(a) ecological overlay

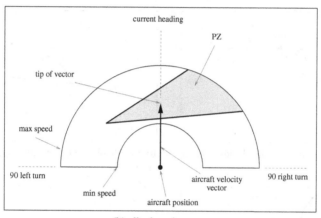

(b) display elements

Fig. 4. Simplified version of the Ecological separation assistance display: the "state-vector" envelope for 2D motion (top); elements of the display (bottom).

The second key element of the display is the triangular-shaped zone[2] that visualizes the set of own aircraft velocity vectors that will result in a conflict with another near-by aircraft. All heading and speed settings of the own aircraft that result in the tip of the velocity vector to be located within this "forbidden beam zone" will be unsafe (functional purpose). Vice versa, all heading and speed settings of the own aircraft that result in a velocity vector tip outside this zone are safe. These constraints to our own aircraft motion are caused by the *other* aircraft, the "external" constraints to flight (abstract function).

With our display, pilots can directly perceive whether they are in conflict, and also that many alternatives exist to avoid the conflict by changing their aircraft

---

[2] The shape of the zone depends on the assumption of the future aircraft trajectories [47].

speed, or heading, or both (generalized function). In the situation illustrated in Fig. 4, pointing the own aircraft velocity vector below the zone (i.e., slow down) means that the other aircraft will eventually pass us in front; pointing the vector above the zone (speed up) means that we will pass the other aircraft in front. We could also choose to maintain current speed, and turn the vector clockwise with, say, 40°, which will also resolve the conflict and have the other aircraft pass us in front. Hence, the display shows the future consequences of our possible actions in a directly perceivable way. It explicitly visualizes the dynamics of relative motion (abstract function) and the ways to fulfill our functional purposes through manipulating this relative motion (generalized function). Our display properly visualizes and connects the means of flying (change heading, speed) with the ends of flight (being safe, productive and efficient), a true ecological interface [21].

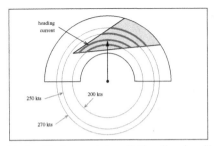

(a) the display contains all "heading band" constraints

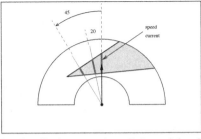

(b) the display contains all "speed band" constraints

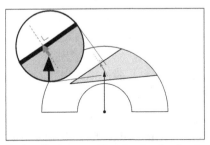

(c) the display specifies the "optimal solution": the smallest state change

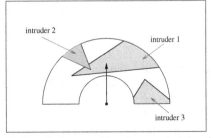

(d) the display specifies the constraints of multiple aircraft conflicts

Fig. 5. Example of how the ecological separation display specifies all the constraints.

Working with this representation led to some important insights. First of all, our display shows the complete "solution space" to pilots, and includes all possible heading bands (see Fig. 5(a)) and speed bands (see Fig. 5(b)) of the traditional design. That is, when reducing speed to, say, 200 kts, and then changing the aircraft heading, the part of the 200 kts-circle that coincides with the forbidden beam zone, equals the heading band computed by the predictive-ASAS algorithm. The forbidden beam zone represents all possible heading bands for this particular conflict, see Fig. 5(a). Similarly, for each possible heading change, like 40° left of the current heading, the part of the 40° line that coincides with the forbidden zone, shows the velocities which lead to a conflict, the speed bands, see Fig. 5(b).

With this visual, *symbolic* presentation of the self-separation situation the pilot can also directly see the optimal solution: the smallest state change of the own velocity vector that will move the tip of the vector outside of the zone, see Fig. 5(c). Here, as shown by the zoomed-in inset of the figure, a small heading change to the left, combined with a small speed increase, will bring the tip of the own aircraft velocity vector outside of the zone, avoiding the conflict; the pilot can also directly see that she will then pass the other aircraft in front.

One of the most interesting characteristics of our display is that, when more aircraft are flying near-by, these may all cause external constraints that limit the own aircraft motion possibilities, limiting the solution space; see Fig. 5(d) for a situation with three other 'intruder' aircraft. In this rather complex situation, which may happen in very dense parts of the airspace, the pilot can directly see that a way to resolve the conflict with intruder #1, one that does not lead to conflicts with the other two intruders, would be to speed up, and move the tip of the velocity vector above the forbidden beam zone caused by the first intruder. He will then pass that aircraft in front, and also pass the other two aircraft in front. Hence, the display is also suitable for resolving multi-aircraft separation problems, although in these cases determining the best, optimal maneuver may be less obvious and could perhaps be found with the help of an automated agent.

Fig. 6. Ecological airborne assistance overlay added to the Navigation Display.

Figure 6 shows the Navigation Display augmented with the ecological overlay at the bottom center. Here we have a conflict with two aircraft (callsigns AA386 and AA387), and one way to solve both conflicts would be to speed up, such that the own aircraft passes both other aircraft in front. Another solution (of many solutions!) would be to speed up a little and turn 30° to the right, such that we pass AA386 in front, and we pass AA387 behind.

5.5   Lessons Learned

When considering the differences between the traditional and ecological designs, the latter is richer and provides more meaningful information about the conflict situation. It allows pilots to quickly obtain a full understanding of the situation, and the visualization of relative motion allows the pilots to directly observe the possibilities for actions and the consequences of taking an action. We think this is what traffic 'situation awareness' is all about.

At the core of the design is the work domain analysis, which helps the analysts and designers to become experts in the problem at hand, understanding the functional means-ends relationships of the system-to-be-built, independent of 'who' or 'what' will do the actual work. It shows what aspects of the work domain are so crucial that they have to be visualized on the display, and will help to explore what possible representations of the world exist and could be used for the system design. The iterations that follow, involving prototyping and testing may lead to novel insights into the problem and may result in adaptations of the analysis, the representation, and the interface.

Note that the ecological interface design does *not* prohibit the use of automated help. *We do not plead against automation.* On the contrary, the ecological interface could well be the "transparent window to the automation" that is mandatory when pilots are responsible to verify an automated agents' advice. The internal and external constraints as visualized on the ecological interface are constraints of "the world" which also hold for automation: the WDA and corresponding ecological interface are actor-independent.

6   Second Example: Separation by Air Traffic Control

Following our work discussed in the first example, we later successfully applied the same concepts to air traffic control. Here, an analysis showed that close to 50% of all short-term conflict alerts are caused by operator's responses to previous alerts [49]. That is, with the current radar-like electronic interface, sketched in the lower left-hand side of Fig. 7, when air traffic controllers 'solve' a conflict (commonly detected first by computer algorithms, which then provide an alert to the controller, who resolves the conflict) their resolution actions trigger new conflicts later. Clearly, an inefficient and ineffective process where much can be gained using, as we will see, only minor changes to the current interface design.

In the lower right corner of Fig. 7 we illustrate our ecological overlay augmented on an experimental ATC radar screen, along with the AH mappings in the upper right corner. When the automation has warned the controller about a predicted loss of separation (i.e., conflict), she can click on one of the aircraft involved, and *directly see* solutions that solve the conflict *and do not lead to new conflicts in the near future*. In Fig. 7, the left aircraft has been selected and reveals its solution space that is restricted by a conflict zone induced by the other aircraft. Any instruction (i.e., speed and/or heading) that brings the speed vector outside the conflict zone would be a valid solution to the conflict. We refer to our interfaces as 'Solution Space Diagrams', SSD for short [50].

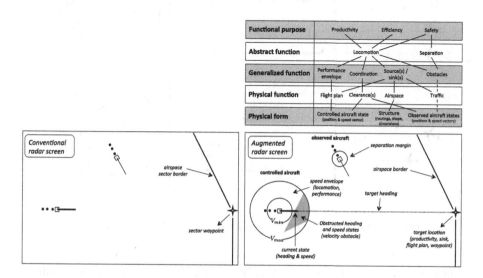

Fig. 7. Evolution of the ecological airborne assistance display to an ecological plan view ATC interface; the Solution Space Diagram (SSD) (adapted from [51]).

In the example shown in Fig. 7, the air traffic controller is solving the conflict in 2D and thereby it is assumed that both aircraft fly on the same flight level. In real-life air traffic control, however, the altitude dimension plays a very important role in safely guiding aircraft towards their destination. In conventional radar displays, controllers can see the altitude of aircraft by inspecting the information shown in their flight labels. Controllers usually inspect the flight labels to discover which aircraft are on the same, or different flight levels, and as such scan for conflicts. Including the altitude dimension in an 'ecological way' on a topdown 2D radar display is not trivial, however.

One concept that remains close to the original solution space method is to filter the conflict zones by relevant flight levels, see Fig. 8 [52]. Here, Fig. 8(a) shows the horizontal and vertical situation of two aircraft flying on the same altitude (A_1 and A_2) and one (A_3) on a different altitude. The right column then shows the solution space when controlling aircraft A_1. Since no vertical

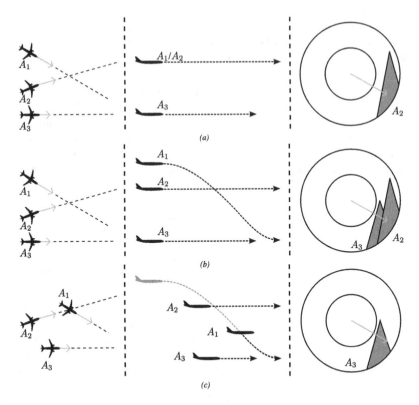

Fig. 8. The SSD with altitude-based filtering (adapted from [52]).

maneuvers are currently performed, only aircraft A_1 and A_2 can be in conflict. In the SSD, only the conflict zone of A_2 shows up.

Figure 8(b) shows another situation, with all three aircraft flying on different altitudes, and where A_1 would start a descent. Here, aircraft A_1 will be crossing the altitudes of both aircraft A_2 and A_3, resulting in both conflict zones being drawn in the SSD. When the situation progresses, see Fig. 8(c), aircraft A_1 will have descended below A_2, and will not be able to get into conflict with A_2 anymore; hence, only the conflict zone of A_3 is shown.

Although the SSD can provide an insight into the traffic situation, the decision on how and when to solve a conflict remains in the hands of the controller. This is especially important for ATC, because research indicated that air traffic controllers are amongst the most critical population in accepting new technology [53]. In the past, many novel tools and technologies, heavily tested in renowned labs, have ultimately not been embraced by the ATC community, simply because controllers did not accept or appreciate them [53]. In many cases, their judgment was fair because the technology would force them to work along a fixed set of strategies and procedures, which goes against some of the main principles of their

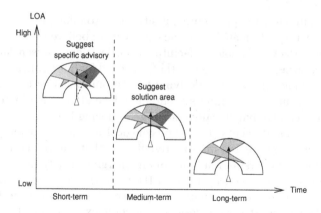

Fig. 9. The compatibility of the SSD with the Levels of Automation (LOA) construct.

current work. In this domain, procedural compliance is often too restrictive in highly dynamic environments featuring uncertainties.

However, the drawback of letting controllers free to choose any strategy they prefer, given it does not violate work domain constraints, also means they could opt for suboptimal strategies. In an effort to make their decisions more efficient, we have augmented the SSD with resolution advisories [51,54]. In Fig. 9 it is illustrated how we made the SSD compatible with the Levels of Automation (LOA) construct as devised by Sheridan, Wickens and Parasuraman [55]. It is a nice example of automation and humans working as a team, and this set-up allows also to move back and forth between several levels of automation authority. That is, one could opt for not only warning the controller, but also presenting a resolution advice to her. When equipped with the solution space overlay, the controller can then check very easily whether the automation advice is correct, and how the traffic situation will emerge in the near future. We are confident that, with the help of our ecological overlays, the 50% of conflict alerts triggered by the controller's earlier responses [49] can be brought down to a minimum, yielding a safer and much more efficient air transport.

7   Closing Statements

In this book chapter we discussed two examples of our work which aims at supporting human operators in safety-critical work. Central in our approach is that we attempt to visualize situations in a meaningful way, such that opera-tors can immediately pick-up the essential ingredients of that situation, and act on it appropriately. The ecological approach to interface design, as advocated by Vicente and Rasmussen in the early 1990s, has been extremely useful. It helped us to search for and capture the essence of what is needed, and construct interfaces and automation tools that reveal this essence, such that human and automated agents can work together. We would like to end this chapter with three closing statements.

First of all, in our attempts to present situations to pilots, it is not our intention to put the automation aside. On the contrary, we believe that our ecological interfaces are perfectly capable to facilitate coordination between humans and automation, creating the transparency that is needed for operators to understand situations and judge the logic underlying the automation's actions or advices. A joint cognitive human-machine system should be strived for in cockpits, in which cognition can be dynamically distributed, moving back and forth between human and automated agents [15]. The ecological interface provides pilots the "window on the world", based on a representation that can be used by humans and automation to understand and act upon emerging situations [16].

Second, a common misconception on EID [56] is that the ecological interface is simple, and easy-to-use, one that quickly turns novices into experts. On the contrary, ecological interfaces are designed for complex work and the complexity of the work domain is reflected by the complexity in the visual interface [57]. Ecological interfaces are made by experts to be used by experts, and it requires the analyst to understand the problem space of the work domain extremely well. That is, in order to construct an EID for a particular problem, the analyst rapidly becomes an expert in this problem herself. This makes EID a rather difficult and sometimes tedious approach to interface design, one that can easily lead to disappointment and failure. Generally speaking, perhaps the approach better fits engineers, as it requires the analyst to focus on the governing (often physical, dynamic) principles of "the world" – the environment in which the brain operates – rather than the brain itself. It requires one to study what's happening *outside* of the human head, not inside.

Finally, when the work domain analysis is done, their is no recipe for creating the actual display itself. In our experience, several iterations are needed, often in combination with human-in-the-loop evaluations of prototypes [4]. Deciding on what system 'state variables' are used to design the interface and automated tools is crucial. Aviation has several examples where, because of (on hindsight) unfortunate design decisions early on in the development of systems – like in autopilots, see [58] – interfaces and automation are not complete. The resulting (human factors) problems will continue to pop up now and then, but the real problem is rooted deeper inside these legacy systems.

Acknowledgments. We would like to acknowledge our graduate students and PhD students from Delft University of Technology who worked with us on further developing and applying ecological approaches to interface design in aviation. Their work efforts contributed greatly to our insights and their enthusiasm continues to be a huge inspiration for us to continue on this track.

References

1. Mulder, M., Borst, C., van Paassen, M.M.: Designing for situation awareness - an aviation perspective. In: Proceedings of the International Conference on Computer-Human Interaction Research and Applications (CHIRA 2017), Funchal, Portugal, pp. 9–20 (2017). ISBN 978-989-758-267-7

2. Vicente, K.J., Rasmussen, J.: The ecology of human-machine systems II: mediating "direct-perception" in complex work domains. Ecol. Psychol. **2**, 207–249 (1990)
3. Vicente, K.J., Rasmussen, J.: Ecological interface design: theoretical foundations. IEEE Trans. Syst. Man Cybern. **22**, 589–606 (1992)
4. Van Paassen, M.M., Borst, C., Ellerbroek, J., Mulder, M., Flach, J.M.: Ecological interface design for vehicle locomotion control. IEEE Trans. Hum.-Mach. Syst. **48**, 541–555 (2018)
5. Endsley, M.: Measurement of situation awareness in dynamic systems. Hum. Factors **37**, 65–84 (1995)
6. Endsley, M.: Toward a theory of situation awareness. Hum. Factors **37**, 32–64 (1995)
7. Breton, R., Rousseau, R.: Situation awareness: a review of the concept and its measurement. Technical report DRDC TR-2001-220, Defence Research and Development Canada - Valcartier (2001)
8. Flach, J.M., Mulder, M., Van Paassen, M.M.: The concept of the situation in psychology. In: Banbury, S., Tremblay, S. (eds.) A Cognitive Approach to Situation Awareness: Theory and Application, pp. 42–60. Ashgate Publishing, Oxon (2004). ISBN 0754641988
9. Vicente, K.J.: Cognitive Work Analysis - Toward Safe, Productive and Healthy Computer-Based Work. Lawrence Erlbaum Associates, Mahwah (1999)
10. Wiener, E.L., Curry, R.E.: Flight-deck automation: promises and problems. Ergonomics **23**, 995–1011 (1980)
11. Billings, C.E.: Aviation Automation - The Search for a Human-Centered Approach. Lawrence Erlbaum Associates Inc., Mahwah (1997)
12. Johnson, S.L., Roscoe, S.N.: What moves, the airplane or the world? Hum. Factors: J. Hum. Factors Ergon. Soc. **14**, 107–129 (1972)
13. Roscoe, S.N., Corl, L., Jensen, R.S.: Flight display dynamics revisited. Hum. Factors **23**, 341–353 (1981)
14. Rasmussen, J.: Skills, rules, and knowledge; signals, signs, and symbols, and other distinctions in human performance models. IEEE Trans. Syst. Man Cybern. **13**, 257–266 (1983)
15. Woods, D.D., Hollnagel, E.: Joint Cognitive Systems: Patterns in Cognitive Systems Engineering. Taylor and Francis, Boca Ratan (2006)
16. Van Paassen, M.M., Borst, C., Klomp, R.E., Mulder, M., Van Leeuwen, P., Mooij, M.: Designing for shared cognition in air traffic management. J. Aerosp. Oper. **2**, 39–51 (2013)
17. Klomp, R.E., Borst, C., Van Paassen, M.M., Mulder, M.: Expertise level, control strategies, and robustness in future air traffic control decision aiding. IEEE Trans. Hum.-Mach. Syst. **46**, 255–266 (2016)
18. Gibson, J.J.: The Senses Considered as Perceptual Systems. Houghton Mifflin, Boston (1966)
19. Gibson, J.J.: The Ecological Approach to Visual Perception. Lawrence Erlbaum Associates, Hillsdale (1986). Originally published in 1979
20. Amelink, M.H.J., Mulder, M., Van Paassen, M.M., Flach, J.M.: Theoretical foundations for a total energy-based perspective flight-path display. Int. J. Aviat. Psychol. **15**, 205–231 (2005)
21. Van Dam, S.B.J., Mulder, M., Van Paassen, M.M.: Ecological interface design of a tactical airborne separation assistance tool. IEEE Trans Syst. Man Cybern. Part A **38**, 1221–1233 (2008)

22. Ellerbroek, J., Visser, M., Van Dam, S.B.J., Mulder, M., Van Paassen, M.M.: Design of an airborne three-dimensional separation assistance display. IEEE Trans. Syst. Man Cybern. Part A **41**, 863–875 (2011)
23. Ellerbroek, J., Brantegem, K.C.R., Van Paassen, M.M., Mulder, M.: Design of a coplanar airborne separation display. IEEE Trans. Hum.-Mach. Syst. **43**, 277–289 (2013)
24. Ellerbroek, J., Brantegem, K.C.R., Van Paassen, M.M., de Gelder, N., Mulder, M.: Experimental evaluation of a coplanar airborne separation display. IEEE Trans. Hum.-Mach. Syst. **43**, 290–301 (2013)
25. Borst, C., Suijkerbuijk, H.C.H., Mulder, M., Van Paassen, M.M.: Ecological interface design for terrain awareness. Int. J. Aviat. Psychol. **16**, 375–400 (2006)
26. Borst, C., Sjer, F.A., Mulder, M., Van Paassen, M.M., Mulder, J.A.: Ecological approach to support pilot terrain awareness after total engine failure. J. Aircr. **45**, 159–171 (2008)
27. Borst, C., Mulder, M., Van Paassen, M.M.: Design and simulator evaluation of an ecological synthetic vision display. J. Guid. Control Dyn. **33**, 1577–1591 (2010)
28. Mulder, M., Winterberg, R., Van Paassen, M.M., Mulder, M.: Direct manipulation interfaces for in-flight four-dimensional navigation. Int. J. Aviat. Psychol. **20**, 249–268 (2010)
29. Van Marwijk, B.J.A., Borst, C., Mulder, M., Mulder, M., Van Paassen, M.M.: Supporting 4D trajectory revisions on the flight deck: design of a human-machine interface. Int. J. Aviat. Psychol. **21**, 35–61 (2011)
30. Tielrooij, M., In't Veld, A.C., Van Paassen, M.M., Mulder, M.: Development of a time-space diagram to assist ATC in monitoring continuous descent approaches. In: Mulder, M. (ed.) Air Traffic Control. SCIYO, pp. 135–147 (2010). ISBN 9789537619-X-X
31. Klomp, R.E., Van Paassen, M.M., Mulder, M., Roerdink, M.I.: Air traffic control interface for creating 4D inbound trajectories. In: Proceedings of the 16th International Symposium on Aviation Psychology (ISAP), Dayton (OH), 2–5 May, pp. 263–268. Wright State University (2011)
32. Van der Eijk, A., Borst, C., In't Veld, A.C., Van Paassen, M.M., Mulder, M.: Assisting air traffic controllers in planning and monitoring continuous-descent approaches. J. Aircr. **49**, 1376–1390 (2012)
33. De Leege, A.M.P., Van Paassen, M.M., Mulder, M.: The time-space diagram as an assistance for ATC in monitoring closed path continuous descent operations. J. Aircr. **50**, 1394–1408 (2013)
34. Fuchs, C., Borst, C., De Croon, G.C.H.E., Van Paassen, M.M., Mulder, M.: An ecological approach to the supervisory control of UAV swarms. Int. J. Micro-Air Veh. **6**, 211–224 (2014)
35. SESAR: Sesar Definition Phase D3: The ATM Target Concept. Technical report no. DLM-0612-001-02-00, EUROCONTROL (2007)
36. Hoekstra, J.M.: Designing for safety: the free flight air traffic management concept. Ph.D. dissertation, Faculty of Technology, Policy and Management, Delft University of Technology (2001)
37. Bainbridge, L.: Ironies of automation. Automatica **19**, 775–779 (1983)
38. Parasuraman, R., Riley, V.A.: Humans and automation: use, misuse, disuse, abuse. Hum. Factors **39**, 230–253 (1997)
39. Rasmussen, J., Pejtersen, A., Goodstein, L.: Cognitive Systems Engineering. Wiley, New York (1994)

40. Van Paassen, M.M., Mulder, M., Van Dam, S.B.J., Amelink, M.H.J.: "Meaningful physics" or finding a system description suitable for ecological interface design. In: Proceedings of the 13th International Symposium on Aviation Psychology, Oklahoma City (OK), USA, 18–21 April, pp. 592–596 (2005)

41. Mulder, M.: Ecological flight deck design: the world behind the glass. In: Viduluch, M.A., Flach, J.M., Tsang, P.S. (eds.) Advances in Aviation Psychology, pp. 103–120. Ashgate (2014). ISBN 978-1-4724-3840-9

42. Ellerbroek, J.: Airborne conflict resolution in three dimensions. Ph.D. dissertation, Faculty of Aerospace Engineering, Delft University of Technology (2013)

43. Tychonievich, L., Zaret, D., Mantegna, J., Evans, R., Muehle, E., Martin, S.: Maneuvering-board approach to path planning with moving obstacles. In: International Joint Conference on Artificial Intelligence, pp. 1017–1021 (1989)

44. Chakravarthy, A., Ghose, D.: Obstacle avoidance in a dynamic environment: a collision cone approach. IEEE Syst. Man Cybern.-Part A: Syst. Hum. **28**, 562–574 (1998)

45. Fiorini, P., Shiller, Z.: Motion planning in dynamic environments using velocity obstacles. Int. J. Robot. Res. **17**, 760–772 (1998)

46. Degré, T., Lefèvre, X.: A collision avoidance system. J. Navig. **34**, 294–302 (1981)

47. Mercado-Velasco, G.A., Borst, C., Ellerbroek, J., Van Paassen, M.M., Mulder, M.: The use of intent information in conflict detection and resolution models based on dynamic velocity obstacles. IEEE Trans. Intell. Transp. Syst. **16**, 2297–2302 (2015)

48. Heylen, F.M., Van Dam, S.B.J., Mulder, M., Van Paassen, M.M.: Design of a vertical separation assistance display. In: Proceedings of the AIAA Guidance, Navigation and Control Conference, Honolulu (HI), USA, 18–21 August (2008)

49. Lillo, F., et al.: Coupling and complexity of interaction of STCA networks. In: Proceedings of the EUROCONTROL Innovative ATM Research Workshop, Brétigny-sur-Orge, France, 1–3 December, EUROCONTROL, pp. 1–12 (2009)

50. Mercado Velasco, G.A., Van Paassen, M.M., Mulder, M.: Analysis of air traffic controller workload reduction based on the solution space for the merging task. In: Proceedings of the AIAA Guidance, Navigation, and Control Conference, Toronto, Canada, 2–5 August, Number AIAA-2010-7541, American Institute for Aeronautics and Astronautics (2010)

51. Borst, C., Bijsterbosch, V.A., Van Paassen, M.M., Mulder, M.: Ecological interface design: supporting fault diagnosis of automated advice in a supervisory air traffic control task. Cogn. Technol. Work **19**, 545–560 (2017)

52. Lodder, J., Comans, J., Van Paassen, M.M., Mulder, M.: Altitude-extended solution space diagram for air traffic controllers. In: Proceedings of the 16th International Symposium on Aviation Psychology (ISAP), Dayton (OH), 2–5 May, pp. 345–350. Wright State University (2011)

53. Westin, C.A.L., Borst, C., Hilburn, B.G.: Strategic conformance: overcoming acceptance issues of decision aiding automation? IEEE Trans. Hum.-Mach. Syst. **46**, 41–52 (2016)

54. Hilburn, B.G., Westin, C.A.L., Borst, C.: Will controllers accept a machine that thinks like they think? The role of strategic conformance in decision aiding automation. Air Traffic Control Q. **22**, 115–136 (2014)

55. Parasuraman, R., Sheridan, T.B., Wickens, C.D.: A model for types and levels of human interaction with automation. IEEE Trans Syst. Man Cybern. Part A **30**, 286–297 (2000)

56. Borst, C., Flach, J.M., Ellerbroek, J.: Beyond ecological interface design: lessons from concerns and misconceptions. IEEE Trans. Hum.-Mach. Syst. **45**, 164–175 (2015)

57. Flach, J.M.: Complexity: learning to muddle through. Cogn. Technol. Work **14**, 187–197 (2012)
58. Lambregts, A.A.: TECS generalized airplane control system design - an update. In: Chu, Q.P., Mulder, J.A., Choukroun, D., van Kampen, E.J., de Visser, C., Looye, G. (eds.) Advances in Aerospace Guidance, Navigation and Control, pp. 503–534. Springer, Berlin (2013). https://doi.org/10.1007/978-3-642-38253-6_30

A Structured Approach for Designing Adaptive Interactive Systems by Unifying Situation-Analytics with Model- and Pattern-Based User Interface Development

Christian Märtin[1(✉)], Christian Herdin[1,2], Jürgen Engel[1,2],
and Felix Kampfer[1]

[1] Faculty of Computer Science, Augsburg University of Applied Sciences,
Augsburg, Germany
{Christian.Maertin, Christian.Herdin, Juergen.Engel,
Felix.Kampfer}@hs-augsburg.de
[2] Institute of Computer Science, University of Rostock, Rostock, Germany

Abstract. This paper discusses the SitAdapt 2.0 development approach for constructing adaptive interactive systems. Resulting applications provide situation-awareness and respond to changing contexts, environments, user emotions, and biometric signals. An observer component is watching the user during interaction with the system. The adaptation process is triggered by situation changes or the recognition of new situations. The necessary software modifications are established in real-time by activating situation rules and exploiting the pattern- and model-based resources of the PaMGIS development framework for model based user interface development. It is shown in detail, how the adaptation process exploits the different PaMGIS models before and during runtime. The SitAdapt approach may also serve for finding user personas, optimizing user experience, and allowing for individualized digital marketing activities. The approach is currently being evaluated for applications from the e-business domain.

Keywords: Situation analytics · Emotion recognition · Adaptive user interfaces · HCI-patterns · Situation rules · Model-based User Interface Design · PaMGIS · CAMELEON reference framework

1 Introduction

Model-based user interface development (MBUID) environments provide model categories and automated tools for building flexible interactive systems that meet both functional and user experience criteria for generic and domain-specific requirements. By exploiting models for specifying the business domain, user tasks, user preferences, dialog and presentation styles, as well as device and platform characteristics, the resulting software apps can be tailored to varying user needs and target environments. Model categories also support user interface design on different refinement levels from highly abstract user interface models to concrete models with specified media and

A. Holzinger et al. (Eds.): CHIRA 2017, CCIS 654, pp. 45–65, 2019.
https://doi.org/10.1007/978-3-030-32965-5_3

interaction objects down to platform and device-specific final user interfaces with precisely defined layout and presentation styles.

Model-based development can also provide the architectural basis for responsive design, by controlling the layout and presentation requirements when migrating from one device type (e.g. desktop) to another (e.g. smartphone) in real-time. In addition, the CAMELEON reference framework [3], a de-facto standard architecture for MBUIDEs also includes model categories that allow for adapting the target software in pre-defined ways before software generation or during runtime.

However, evolution in software engineering is progressing rapidly and recently has led to the emergence of intelligent applications that observe the users' emotions – together with the changing interaction context – in order to better understand the individual users' feelings and behavior. The principal goal from an HCI perspective is to reach improved user experience and task accomplishment by letting the software react and adapt to changing individual users' needs in real-time.

In other words, the interaction context, both within the application and the real world environment of the users is analyzed and the users' situation is recognized by such intelligent monitoring systems. The term situation analytics [4] was coined to stimulate the development of sound software engineering approaches for developing and running such situation-aware adaptive systems that ultimately also recognize the mostly hidden mental state of the system users and are able to react to it.

In this paper, which is an extended version of [13], we present a new approach for building situation-analytic capabilities and real-time adaptive behavior into interactive applications that were designed by MBUID frameworks. With SitAdapt 2.0 we introduce the full implementation of our runtime-architecture and we demonstrate, how model-based design can fruitfully be combined with synchronized multi-channel emotion recognition and eye-tracking software that is used to trigger the real-time adaptation of the interactive target application by exploiting pattern and model repositories at runtime. The main contributions of this paper are the following:

- Design of architecture extensions for an existing MBUID framework for enabling real-time adaptation of target application user interfaces by using situation analytics
- Discussion of the use of situation-awareness and HCI patterns for adaptation purposes
- Detailed discussion of the adaptation process with the focus on user-related adaptations.

In addition to [13] we discuss the following new topics:

- The SitAdapt 2.0 situation-rules with a new rule editor for defining situation/action rules that can trigger the adaption process at runtime
- The structural relations and dynamic interactions between the various models of the MBUID framework and the SitAdapt interpreter
- New application examples that demonstrate the impact of situation-based adaptation on the user interface and the application
- Broader and improved discussion of the related work in the fields of context-awareness and adaptive systems.

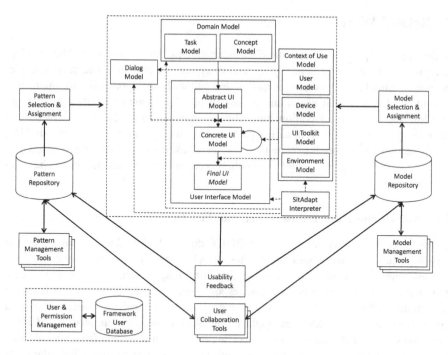

Fig. 1. Overview of the PaMGIS development framework with the integrated SitAdapt interpreter component and its communication paths. The figure was extracted from [13]. New communication paths were added.

The paper is organized in the following way. Section 2 discusses related work in the field of model- and pattern-based user interface development systems and defines the underlying concept of "situation". The section also discusses the related work in the areas of situation-aware systems, model and pattern based construction of interactive systems, and emotion recognition with visual, biometric and browser-only data.

Section 3 introduces the SitAdapt Interpreter. SitAdapt 2.0., the current implementation of our approach for developing and running situation-analytic adaptive interactive systems is discussed. The section starts with an overview of the architecture and components of the system and after this focuses on discussing the adaptation process and the various adaptation types supported by the system in detail. The PPSL specification language for HCI-patterns and model fragments used in the process is discussed elsewhere [6].

Section 4 demonstrates the SitAdapt interpreter at work. It gives an example for a recognized situation that leads to adaptations of the system that require interaction with models for the more abstract user interface and application models as well as for the final user interface.

Section 5 concludes the paper with a short discussion of currently evolving target applications, the data mining process for guiding browser-only situation-recognition with data extracted by the SitAdapt interpreter, and gives hints to our planned future work.

2 Related Work

In this paper we present the user interface adaptation process controlled by the SitAdapt interpreter and discuss the underlying overall system architecture. The current implementation, SitAdapt 2.0, combines model- and pattern-based approaches for interactive system construction with visual and bio-signal-based emotion recognition technology to allow for software adaptation by real-time situation analytics. The software and monitoring technology used in earlier prototypes of the system was introduced in [15]. In this section we explore the related work in the areas of model- and pattern-based user interface design, situation analytics, emotion recognition, and adaptation to changing contexts.

2.1 Model- and Pattern-Based User Interface Design

Model-based User Interface Design (MBUID) during the last decades has paved the way for many well-structured approaches, development environments and tools for building high-quality interactive systems that fulfill tough requirements regarding user experience, platform-independence, and responsiveness. Model-based approaches have also improved the coordinated evolutionary development of both the business logic and the interactive parts of complex applications. Within software engineering MBUID techniques have a long tradition for supporting the smooth transition from very abstract early raw business models to fully equipped interactive apps by controlling the mappings from all parts of the user interface models and the resulting final user interface to the business models and the resulting final core logic throughout the whole software life-cycle [14].

At the same time model-driven and model-based architectural and development approaches [16] were introduced to automate parts of the development process and shorten time-to-market for flexible interactive software products. As one de-facto process and architectural standard for MBUID the CAMELEON reference framework has emerged [3]. CRF defines many model categories and a comprehensive base architecture for the construction of powerful model-based development environments.

In order to allow for automation of the development process for interactive systems, to raise the quality and user experience levels of the resulting application software and to stimulate developer creativity, many software-pattern-based design approaches were introduced in the HCI field during the last 15 years [2].

In order to get the best results from both, model and pattern-based approaches, the SitAdapt interpreter is integrated into the PaMGIS (Pattern-Based Modeling and Generation of Interactive Systems) development framework [6, 7], which is based on the CAMELEON reference framework (CRF). PaMGIS contains all models proposed by CRF, but also exploits pattern-collections for modeling and code generation. The CRF is guiding the developer on how to transform an abstract user interface over intermediate model artifacts into a final user interface. The overall structure of the PaMGIS framework with its tools and resources, the incorporated CRF models, and the new SitAdapt interpreter is shown in Fig. 1.

The SitAdapt interpreter component has access to the domain model, to all sub-models of the context of use model (context model), the dialog model and mainly interacts with the user interface model.

Within CRF-conforming systems the abstract user interface model (AUI) is generated from the information contained in the domain model of the application that includes a task model and a concept model (i.e. typically an object-oriented class model defining business objects and their relations) and defines abstract user interface objects that are still independent of the context of use.

The AUI model can then be transformed into a concrete user interface model (CUI), which already exploits the context model and the dialog model, which is responsible for the dynamic user interface behavior.

In the next step PaMGIS automatically generates the final user interface model (FUI) by parsing the CUI model. To produce the actual user interface, the resulting XML-conforming UI-specification can either be compiled or interpreted during runtime, depending on the target platform. Section 3 discusses in detail, how the SitAdapt interpreter complements and accesses the PaMGIS framework.

2.2   Context- and Situation-Awareness

Since the advent of smart mobile devices, HCI research has started to take into account the various new usability requirements of application software running on smaller devices with touch-screen or speech interaction or of apps that migrate smoothly from one device type to another. Several of the needed characteristics for these apps targeted at different platforms and devices can be specified and implemented using the models and patterns residing in advanced MBUID systems. Even runtime support for responsiveness with the interactive parts distributed or migrating from one (virtual) machine to the other and the domain objects residing in the cloud can be modeled and managed by CRF-conforming development environments, e.g. [17].

The concept of context-aware computing was originally proposed for distributed mobile computing in [24]. In addition to software and communication challenges to be solved when dynamically migrating an application to various devices and locations within a distributed environment, the definition of context also included environmental and social aspects (e.g. lighting and sound environment, are there other people around?, who are these people? etc.).

At the same time period early definitions of the term situation-awareness appeared in psychology and the cognitive sciences, with the aim to support human operators in complex situations, e.g. pilots during the landing phase, by defining situation-dependent requirements for allowing a smooth and correct task accomplishment [8, 9]. The main focus of these approaches that have heavily affected human-machine system development and the design of socio-technical systems during the last decades, lies in using advanced automation and visualization tools for letting the operator (e.g. a jet pilot) easily recognize the specific current situation and giving her support for successfully handling this situation with the right tools and information [19].

With a rising level of machine intelligence the borderline between a human operator, who recognizes a situation, because the software system provides the needed visualization and data, or a technical system that recognizes the situation and acts on its own behalf, is flexible, as demonstrated by the current advances in autonomous driving systems.

It is a fact that during recent years mobile software has made huge steps towards understanding of and reacting to varying situations. To capture the individual requirements of a situation [4] proposed that a situation consists of an environmental context E that covers the user's operational environment, a behavioral context B that covers the user's social behavior by interpreting his or her actions, and a hidden context M that includes the users' mental states and emotions. A situation Sit at a given time t can thus be defined as $Sit = <M, B, E>_t$. A user's intention for using a specific software service for reaching a goal can then be formulated as temporal sequence $<Sit_1, Sit_2, \ldots, Sit_n>$, where Sit_1 is the situation that triggers the usage of a service and Sit_n is the goal-satisfying situation. In [5] the Situ framework is presented that allows the situation-based inference of the hidden mental states of users for detecting the users intentions and identifying their goals. The framework can be used for modeling and implementing applications that are situation aware and adapt themselves to the users' changing needs over runtime.

Our own work, described in the following sections, was inspired by Situ, but puts most emphasis on maintaining the model-based approach of the PaMGIS framework by linking the domain and user interface models with the user-centric situation-aware adaptation component.

An approach for enabling rich personal analytics for mobile applications by defining a specific architectural layer between the mobile apps and the mobile OS platform is proposed in [12]. The new layer allows to access all sensors and low-level I/O-features of the used devices.

By evaluating mouse- and eye-tracking events concurrently in a Web-browser, and by comparing the mouse- and gaze-related metrics, [20] could demonstrate that browser-only observation can detect pleasantness experience 15% better than chance and thus can lead to exploitable results for controlling website content and layout dynamically, e.g. for the placement of advertisements.

The users' reactions to being confronted with the results of a hyper-personal analytics system and the consequences for sharing such information and for privacy are discussed in [27].

For implementing the emotion recognition functionality that can be exploited for inferring the desires and sentiments of individual users while working with the interactive application, the current version of SitAdapt captures both visual and biometric data signals. In [11] we discuss the interplay of the various recognition approaches used in our system.

In [22] an overview of the potential of various emotion recognition technologies in the field of affective computing is given. In [25] emotion recognition technologies based on bio-signals are discussed, whereas [23] discusses the evolution of visual emotion recognition approaches including the interpretation of facial macro- and micro-expressions.

2.3   Context-Adaptation

When using situation analytics for controlling dynamic adaptation, the recognition of emotions and the inference of sentiments and mental states from emotional and other data provide the basis for suggesting adaptive changes of the content, behavior, and the user interface of the target application. In general, three different types of adaptation can be distinguished when focusing on user interfaces [1, 28]:

- Adaptable user interfaces. The user interface is a-priori customized to the personal preferences of the user.
- Semi-automated adaptive user interfaces. The user interface provides recommendations for adaptations, which can be accepted by the user or not.
- Automated adaptive user interfaces. The user interface automatically reacts to changes in the context of the interactive application.

The SitAdapt runtime-architecture co-operates with the PaMGIS framework to support both, semi-automated and automated user interface adaptation. For constructing real situation-aware systems, however, user interface adaptation aspects have to be mixed with content-related static and dynamic system aspects that are typically covered by the task and context model, both together forming the domain model of the framework.

If the set of possible situations that may arise is manageable, an MBUID framework can have the necessary resources for user interface and behavior adaptation available in repositories. SitAdapt distinguishes between situation rules and HCI-pattern- and model-based resources. Situation rules consist of a condition-part defining a situation and actions for adapting the target application. Situation rules may trigger structural, layout, presentational, and behavioral changes of the user interface, ask the user for interactive input, or can even lead to modifications of the internal structure and behavior of the underlying domain model. Situation rules may activate user interface building resources, e.g. HCI-patterns or model fragments, within the PaMGIS environment.

Such HCI-pattern- and model-based resources are stored within the PaMGIS model- and pattern-repositories in the form of PPSL specifications that can be exploited for code generation at runtime [6].

If the set of possible situations is not clearly limited or if new and unforeseen situations arise, a learning component that creates new situation rules will become a necessary component of the adaptive system. Rule-based evolutionary learning systems as used in organic computing could also be helpful for adapting interactive systems to new situations arising by observing unforeseen mixes or temporal changes of the emotional state and the work context [26].

In [18] a taxonomy for classifying and comparing the key-concepts of diverse approaches for implementing context-awareness is presented. The paper gives a good overview of the current state-of-the-art in this field.

3 SitAdapt – Architecture

In order to profit from earlier results in the field of MBUID systems, the SitAdapt runtime environment is integrated into the PaMGIS (Pattern-Based Modeling and Generation of Interactive Systems) development framework. The SitAdapt environment extends the PaMGIS framework and allows for modeling context changes in the user interface in real-time.

The architecture (Fig. 3) consists of the following parts:

- The *data interfaces* from the different devices (eye-tracker, wristband, facial expression recognition, metadata from the application).
- The *recording component* that synchronizes the different input records with a timestamp. The component also records the eye- and gaze-tracking signal of the user and tracks his or her emotional video facial expression with the Noldus Face-Reader software as a combination of the six basic emotions (happy, sad, scared, disgusted, surprised, and angry). Other recorded data about the user are, e.g., age-range and gender. The stress-level and other biometric data are recorded in real-time by a wristband. In addition, mouse movements and keyboard logs are protocolled.
- The *database writer* stores the data from the recording component and from the browser in the database and manages the communication with the rule editor.

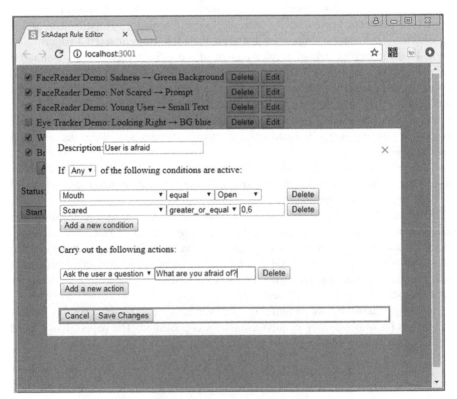

Fig. 2. SitAdapt 2.0 rule editor.

- The *rule editor* allows the definition and modification of situation rules, e.g. for specifying the different user states (e.g. if an angry state is observed, it will only become relevant, if the state lasts more than five seconds and the grade of the emotion surpasses a certain activation level). Figure 2 shows the creation of a simple situation rule with two conditions and one action. In this case none of the PaMGIS models is affected and only a dialog with the user is created. However, situation rules can also activate HCI-patterns in the pattern repository. These patterns are exploited by the PaMGIS framework at runtime to generate user interface adaptations from predefined UI-, task-, or domain-model fragments.
- The *situation analytics component* analyzes and assesses situations by exploiting the observed data.
- The *evaluation and decision component* uses the data that are provided by the situation analytics component to decide whether an adaptation of the user interface is currently meaningful and necessary. For this purpose the component evaluates so-called situation rules. Whether an adaptation is meaningful depends on the predefined purpose of the situation-aware target application. Goals to meet can range from successful marketing activities in e-business, e.g. having the user buying an item from the e-shop or letting her or him browse through the latest special offers, to improved user experience levels, or to meeting user desires defined by the hidden mental states of the user. Such goals can be detected, if one or more situations in the situation profile trigger an application dependent or domain independent situation rule. Situation rules are related to patterns. They define behavioral and context-related patterns and therefore are also located in the pattern repository. If the decision component decides that an adaptation is necessary, it has to provide the artifacts from the PaMGIS pattern and model repositories to allow for the modification of the target application by the adaptation component. The situation rules provide the links and control information for accessing and composing HCI-patterns and model fragments, necessary for constructing the modifications. Examples are given in Sect. 4.
- The adaptation component finally generates the necessary modifications of the interactive target application.

These architectural components provided by the SitAdapt system are necessary for enabling the PaMGIS framework to support automated adaptive user interfaces.

3.1 User Interface Construction

The *domain model* (see Fig. 1) serves as the starting point of the process that is used for user interface modeling and generation. The model consists of two sub-models, the *task model* and the *concept model*. The task model is specified using the *ConcurTaskTree (CTT)* notation [21] as well as an XML file, the *UI configuration file*, generated from the CTT description and from accessing contents of the context of use model (see Fig. 1). The concept model id based on the task model and includes the dataobjects (a list of abstract user interface (AUI)-objects). The *context of use model* holds four sub-models: the user model, the device model, the UI toolkit model, and the environment model. All models play important roles in the user interface construction process and are exploited when modeling responsiveness and adapting the target application to specific device types and platforms. For the situation-aware adaptation process, however, the user model is the most relevant of these sub-models.

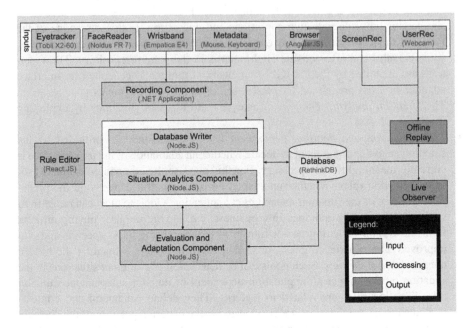

Fig. 3. SitAdapt 2.0 architecture.

It is structured as follows:

```
<UserCharacteristics>
        <UserIdentData>
        <UserAbilities>
                <USRUA_Visual>
                <USRUA_Acoustic>
                <USRUA_Motor>
                <USRUA_Mental>
        <UserExperiences>
                <USRUE_Domain>
                <USRUE_Handling>
        <UserDistraction>
        <UserLegalCapacity>
        <UserEmotionalState>
        <UserPsychologicalState>
        <UserBiometricState>
                <USRBS_Pulse>
                <USRBS_Attention>
                <USRBS_PulseChangeRate>
                ...
```

The *user model* holds both, static information about the current user, and dynamic data describing the emotional and psychological state as well as the biometric state.

Not all of the attributes need to be filled with concrete data values. The dynamic values concerning emotional, biometric, and psychological state are taken from the *situation profile,* whenever an adaptation decision has to be made (see Sect. 3.2). Note, however, that the situation profile that is generated by the situation analytics component is based on the whole sequence of emotional and biometric user states from session start until session termination. The temporal granularity of the situation profile is variable, starting from fractions of a second. It depends on the target application's requirements.

A priori information can be exploited for tailoring the target application, when modeling and designing the appearance and behavior of the user interface, before generating it for the first time and use. This can already be seen as part of the adaptation process.

Typical a priori data can be user identification data, data about the various abilities of the user, and specific data about the users fluency with the target application's domain and its handling.

Dynamic data will change over time and can be exploited for adapting the user interface at runtime. Such data includes the emotional state, biometric state, psychological state observed and measured by the hard- and software devices attached to the recording component.

The data structure also allows to directly use proprietary data formats provided by the devices used in SitAdapt such as the Empatica E4 wrist band.

If not available a priori, some of the attributes can be completed by SitAdapt, after an attribute value was recognized by the system. For instance the age of a user can be determined with good accuracy by the FaceReader software. With this information, the <UserLegalCapacity> attribute can be automatically filled in.

The generated *UI configuration file* contains a <ContextOfUse> tag field for each task. It has sub-tags that may serve as context variables that hold information relevant for controlling the UI configuration and later, at runtime, the adaptation process.

One of the sub-tags may for instance hold information that a task "ticket sale" is only authorized for users from age 18. When the situation analytics component at runtime discovers that the current user is less than 18 years old, a hint is given in the final user interface (FUI) model that she or he is not authorized to buy a ticket, because of her or his age.

The *concept model* consists of the high-level specifications of all the data elements and interaction objects from the underlying business model that are relevant for the user interface. It can be seen as an interface between the business core models of an application and the user interface models. It can be modeled using UML class diagram notation. An XML specification is also derived from the concept model.

In PaMGIS the *task model* serves as the primary basis for constructing the *dialog model* (see Fig. 1). The various dialogs are derived from the tasks of the task model. Additional input for modeling data types and inter-class-relations is provided by the *concept model*. The dialog model is implemented by using Dialog Graphs [10].

In the next step the *abstract user interface (AUI)* is constructed by using the input of the concept model. The dialog model provides the fundamental input for AUI to CUI transformation specification, because it is based on the user tasks. Each of the different dialogs is denoted as a <Cluster>-element. All elements together compose a <Cluster> that is also specified in XML.

For transforming the AUI into *concrete user interface (CUI)* the AUI elements are mapped to <Form> CUI elements. The context of use model is exploited during this transformation. For instance by accessing the UI toolkit sub-model it can be guaranteed that only such widget types are used in the CUI that come with the used toolkit and for which the fitting code can later be generated in conjunction with the target programming or markup language used for the final user interface.

The CUI specification is also written in XML.

Finally, the CUI specification has to be transformed into the *final user interface (FUI)*. The XML specification is therefore parsed and translated into the target language, e.g., HTML, C# or Java.

3.2   User Interface Adaptation Process

For modeling a situation-aware adaptive target application, SitAdapt components are involved in several parts of the entire adaptation process.

Even before the final user interface is generated and displayed for the first time, the situation can be analyzed by SitAdapt. SitAdapt can access the user attributes in the profiles. The observed and synchronized data streams are delivered to the situation analytics component by the database writer. The database writer fetches them from the database. The situation analytics component then stores the analyzed data in the situation profile.

Thus, the user will get an adapted version of the user interface with its first display, but will not notice that an adaptation has already occurred.

At runtime the situation is permanently controlled by the analytics component. In addition, environmental data, e.g. time of day, room lighting, age and gender of the user, emotional level, stress level, etc. can be recorded and pre-evaluated and be attached to the situations in the situation profile.

A situation profile has the following structure:

```
<SituationProfile>
    <TargetApplication>
    <User>
    <Situation_0>
            <SituationTime> 0
            <AUI_link> AUI_object_x
            <CUI_link> CUI_object_x
            <FUI_link> FUI_object_x
            <Dailog_link>
            <Task_link>
            <Concept_link>
            <Eye_Tracking> …
            <Gaze_Tracking> …
            <MetaData> NULL
            <Environment>
                    <EnvAttrib_1> …
                    …
            <EmotionalState> EmoValue_1
            <BiometricState> BioValue_1
                    …
            <EmotionalState> angry
            <BiometricState>
                    <StressLevel> yellow
    …
```

This is the structure of the situation profile as currently used for applications and for evaluating our approach. The attribute <FUI_link> is used to identify the part of the user interface in the focus of the user. For more advanced adaptation techniques additional attributes may be required (see Sect. 3.3). Situations with their attributes provide a dynamic data base for allowing the decision component to find one or more domain dependent or independent situation rules in the pattern repository that match an individual situation or a sequential part of the situation profile. The situation rules hold links to HCI-patterns or model fragments that are used for adaptation purposes.

Typically not all of the existing situation attributes are needed to find a suitable situation rule.

Also note that some situation attributes are not type-bound. The eye- and gaze-tracking attributes, for instance, can either contain numeric coordinates or sequences of such coordinates to allow for analyzing rapidly changing eye movements in fine-grained situation profiles, e.g. when observing a car driver. However, they can also give already pre-processed application-dependent descriptions of the watched UI objects and the type of eye movements (e.g. a repeating loop between two or more visual objects).

To enable adaptations, some modeling aspects of the PaMGIS framework have to be extended.

When transforming the AUI model into the CUI model the current situation profile of the user is checked by the decision component. The situational data in the profile may match domain independent or application specific situation rules. If one or more situation rules apply, these rules guide, how a dynamically adapted CUI can be constructed. The construction information is provided by HCI-patterns and/or model fragments in the PaMGIS repositories. Each situation rule is linked with such UI-defining artifacts.

Situation rules are key resources for the SitAdapt adaptation process. Domain independent situation rules cover recurring standard situations in the user interface. Application-specific situation rules have to be defined and added to the pattern repository when modeling a new target application. They mainly cover aspects that concern specific communications between business objects and the user interface. Existing application-specific situation rules can be reused, if they also apply for a new target application.

The CUI that was modified with respect to the triggering situation then serves as construction template from which the FUI is generated.

However, the FUI is also monitored by SitAdapt at runtime, after it was generated, i.e. when the user interacts with the interactive target application. Thus, the characteristics of the FUI can be modified dynamically by SitAdapt whenever the decision component assesses the occurred situational changes for the user as significant (i.e. the user gets angry or has not moved the mouse for a long time period).

In this case a flag in the UI tells SitAdapt, which part of the AUI (and other model fragments) is responsible for the recognized situation within a window, dialog, widget and/or the current interaction in the FUI. Depending on the situation analytics results, the detected situation rules will hint to the available HCI patterns, model fragments and construction resources (e.g. reassuring color screen background, context-aware tool tip, context-aware speech output, etc.). The decision component may thus trigger a modification of the concerned CUI parts.

The adaptation component then accesses and activates the relevant HCI-patterns and/or model fragments. From the modified CUI a new version of the FUI is generated and displayed, as soon as possible. After adaptation the FUI is again monitored by the situation analytics component.

3.3   Advanced Adaptation Techniques

Two major goals of adaptive technologies are (1) to raise the effectiveness of task accomplishment and (2) to raise the level of user experience. With the resources, tools, and components available in PaMGIS and SitAdapt we are also able to address these goals.

To monitor task accomplishment, links between the sequence of situations in the situation profile and the tasks in the task model have to be established. For this purpose the situation analytics component can access to the task model. As the tasks and subtasks of the task model are related to business objects, the linking of situations to data objects in the concept model can be helpful. With these new communication mechanisms, we can check, whether the sequence of situations goes along with the planned sequence of tasks. If derivations or unforeseen data values occur, situation-aware adaptation can help the user to find back to the intended way.

Both, for situation sequences matching with the task sequences planned by the developer, and for situations that have left the road to the hoped-for business goal, emotional and stress-level monitoring may trigger adaptations of the user interface that raise the joy of use or take pressure from the user in complex situational contexts.

Monitoring different users with SitAdapt while working on the tasks of various target applications in the usability lab can also lead to identifying different personas and usage patterns of the target applications. The findings can also be used for a priori adaptations in the target systems in the case where no situation analytics process is active.

4 SitAdapt in Action

In the following we present some recent examples from our work with SitAdapt.

4.1 Accessing User Interface Models

This simple example demonstrates the functionality of the SitAdapt system for an interactive travel-booking application.

A user will book a trip from one city to another on a booking website. This website applies several HCI-patterns for the booking process. When using SitAdapt for an existing proprietary web-application, a simplified user interface model of the application as well as a task model fragment can be provided in order to make the adaptation functionality partly available for the existing software.

In the first step (Fig. 4) the traveller has to enter her or his personal details into the wizard fields.

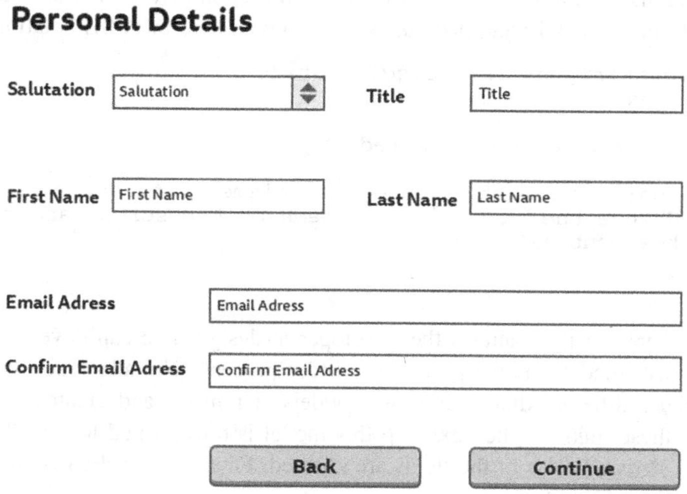

Fig. 4. Personal details wizard.

SitAdapt is monitoring the user during this task. The SitAdapt system records the eye movements, pulse, stress level, psychological state, and the emotional state, and gets real-time information from the website (model links). The situation analytics component creates a user-specific situation from the collected data and analyzes these data:

```
<SituationProfile>
        <TargetApplication>
        <User>
        <Situation_booking>
                <SituationTime> 30 s
                <FUI_link> Wizard_Part_1
                <AUI_link> model_AUI_1
                <CUI_link> model_CUI_1
                <Dialog_link> order_ticket
                <Task_link> order_ticket
                <Concept_link> concept_1
                <Eye_Tracking>
                <EmotionalState>
                <UserPsychologicalState> tired
                <BiometricState>
                        <Pulse> normal
                        <StressLevel> orange
        </Situation_booking>
```

The decision component determines, whether an adaptation is necessary with the help of the pattern repository and the model repository. In this example, a situation rule can be found, that decides that the user is tired. The action part of the rule activates the domain-independent HCI-pattern *tired*, which is given here in PPSL notation:

```
<CLSS_PatternType> PsychologicalState
<Name> tired
...
        <Problem> User is tired
        ...
        <Solution> Reduction of the elements on the screen.
        Change the size of  the items on the screen and change
        the contrast
        ...
```

With the help of this pattern, the developer at design time can develop a second dialog and task model for this part of the order process. The adaptation component looks for these different dialog and task models at runtime and creates a new AUI model with these links. In the next step this model is transformed to the CUI. In this process, the size and color of the fields are adapted. Finally a new FUI is created from this information (Fig. 5).

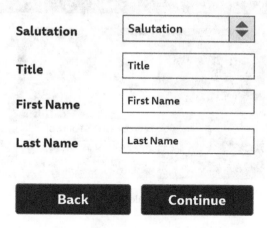

Fig. 5. Adapted personal details wizard.

4.2 Involving the User

To evaluate the SitAdapt 2.0 system, we developed a travel-booking web application to test and highlight some of the system's capabilities. The application features elements typical for e-commerce applications, including the ability to enter query parameters, viewing and selecting query results, viewing product details, registering as a new user, logging in, modifying a selected product, and viewing a summary of all entered data before making a purchase.

Having the ability to collect information about a user's physical and physiological properties allows application designers to offer products and product enrichment opportunities ("extras") that focus on the user's immediate and/or long-term needs, benefitting producers and consumers. In the field of air travel, for instance, knowledge of a user's demographic and his or her current disposition can influence the kinds of seat and airline upgrade opportunities offered to the user.

In Fig. 6 the system can recognize fear, anger, or a higher pulse while a user is in the process of choosing a flight. In response, it offers an effective remedy to combat the customer's fear of flying and/or other negative flight-associated emotions.

Fig. 6. Offering an additional meal service.

In the next example (Fig. 7a, b), the system uses a demographic-focused approach to determine positive flight-related desires and presents an option to fulfill these desires to the user. A user between the ages of 15 and 40 may be presented with an option to purchase Wi-Fi access, while for users with an age over 50 a seat upgrade opportunity may be presented to increase their level of comfort throughout the flight.

Additional sensor information can be used to make predictions about the likelihood of users taking advantage of these product enrichment opportunities. Eye tracking and browser-based mouse-tracking data can offer information about a customer's financial flexibility as they consider or reconsider their budgetary restrictions when looking at the different opportunities.

Fig. 7. (a) Offering Wi-Fi upgrade for young passengers. (b) Offering more legroom for senior citizens.

The SitAdapt system's capabilities are not limited to targeted advertising. Application developers could also use our system to change color schemes to appeal to the user's current mood, change layouts to suit demographic-based technological prowess, change styles to suit possible accessibility needs, record specific diagnostic information and offer help (or ask for specific feedback) when a user becomes frustrated with a certain feature.

4.3   Accessing the Task Model

In this situation rule SitAdapt recognizes the user's interest in a certain product in a web-shop. After two minutes a text is displayed, e.g. notifying the user that in case of the purchase of product (Id) within the next 10 min, a voucher of $20 is granted for the user's next purchase. A link to the voucher-processing task in the task model is activated.

```
<SituationRule> OfferingVoucher
        FOR N <Situation₁> IN 120s
        <Eye_Tracking> Field Product Product(Id)
        <Gaze_Tracking> Contains Field
        Product(Id) (>5)
        <Pulse> (85-100)
        <PulseRate> rising
        <Emotion> excited
        <StressLevel> orange
        <Action> SHOW AT 180s VoucherText1FUI
        <Action> WAIT VoucherText1FUIInput
        <Action> LINK VoucherText1FUIInput
                TaskModel VoucherProcessingTask
```

5   Conclusion

In this paper we have presented SitAdapt 2.0 and the new adaptive functionality developed for the PaMGIS MBUID framework. The new situation interpreter component could be integrated seamlessly into the model- and pattern-based development environment, thereby enabling new runtime features.

SitAdapt is now fully operational. After finalizing the signal synchronization and recording components, the system is currently being tested and evaluated with target applications from the e-business domain. In one realistic application domain we use SitAdapt to watch the user and search for recurring situation rules in the domain of ticket sale for long-distance-travel.

In another domain area we are currently examining, we are evaluating the impact of digital marketing activities on the users of the e-business portal of a cosmetics manufacturer. In our study with eight female test persons we make extensive use of usability-lab based user tests with varying scenarios in order to get sufficient data for mining typical application-dependent situation rules.

As an early result we found out that negative emotions (sadness, anger) in several business-relevant cases helped to identify severe usability issues resulting from user-distraction caused by unfavorable advertisement placement.

For both target application domains we are currently exploring usability, user experience and marketing aspects. It is our next goal to define a large set of situation rules, both domain-dependent and universally applicable and thus stepwise improve the intelligence level and variety of the resources of the SitAdapt decision component.

Acknowledgements. The authors want to express many thanks to Lionnelle Biawan Yameni, who with her B.Sc. thesis heavily contributed to the implementation of the travel-booking demonstrator application for SitAdapt 2.0.

References

1. Akiki, P.A., et al.: Integrating adaptive user interface capabilities in enterprise applications. In: Proceedings of the 36th International Conference on Software Engineering (ICSE 2014), pp. 712–723. ACM (2014)
2. Breiner, K., et al. (eds.): PEICS: towards HCI patterns into engineering of interactive systems. In: Proceedings of the PEICS 2010, pp. 1–3. ACM (2010)
3. Calvary, G., Coutaz, J., Bouillon, L., et al.: The CAMELEON Reference Framework (2002). http://giove.isti.cnr.it/projects/cameleon/pdf/CAMELEON%20D1.1RefFramework.pdf. Accessed 25 Aug 2016
4. Chang, C.K.: Situation analytics: a foundation for a new software engineering paradigm. IEEE Comput. **14**, 24–33 (2016)
5. Chang, C.K., et al.: Situ: a situation-theoretic approach to context-aware service evolution. IEEE Trans. Serv. Comput. **2**(3), 261–275 (2009)
6. Engel, J., Märtin, C., Forbrig, P.: A concerted model-driven and pattern-based framework for developing user interfaces of interactive ubiquitous applications. In: Proceedings of the First International Workshop on Large-Scale and Model-Based Interactive Systems, Duisburg, pp. 35–41 (2015)
7. Engel, J., Märtin, C., Forbrig, P.: Practical aspects of pattern-supported model-driven user interface generation. In: Kurosu, M. (ed.) HCI 2017. LNCS, vol. 10271, pp. 397–414. Springer, Cham (2017). https://doi.org/10.1007/978-3-319-58071-5_30
8. Flach, J.M.: Situation awareness: the emperor's new clothes. In: Mouloua, M., Parasuaman, R. (eds.) Human Performance in Automated Systems: Current Research and Trends, Erlbaum, pp. 241–248 (1994)
9. Flach, J.M., Mulder, M., Van Paassen, M.M.: The concept of the situation in psychology. In: Banbury, S., Tremblay, S. (eds.) A Cognitive Approach to Situation Awareness: Theory and Applications, pp. 42–60. Ashgate Publisching, Oxon (2004)
10. Forbrig, P., Reichart, D.: Spezifikation von „Multiple User Interfaces" mit Dialoggraphen. In: Proc. INFORMATIK 2007: Informatik trifft Logistik, Beiträge der 37. Jahrestagung der Gesellschaft für Informatik e.V. (GI), Bremen (2007)
11. Herdin, C., Märtin, C., Forbrig, P.: SitAdapt: an architecture for situation-aware runtime adaptation of interactive systems. In: Kurosu, M. (ed.) HCI 2017. LNCS, vol. 10271, pp. 447–455. Springer, Cham (2017). https://doi.org/10.1007/978-3-319-58071-5_33
12. Lee, Y., Balan, R.K.: The case for human-centric personal analytics. In: Proceedings of the WPA 2014, pp. 25–29. ACM (2014)
13. Märtin, C., Herdin, C., Engel, J.: Model-based user-interface adaptation by exploiting situations, emotions and software patterns. In: Proceedings of the CHIRA 2017, Funchal, Madeira, 31 October–2 November, SCITEPRESS (2017)
14. Märtin, C., Herdin, C., Engel, J.: Patterns and models for automated user interface construction – in search of the missing links. In: Kurosu, M. (ed.) HCI 2013. LNCS, vol. 8004, pp. 401–410. Springer, Heidelberg (2013). https://doi.org/10.1007/978-3-642-39232-0_44

15. Märtin, C., Rashid, S., Herdin, C.: Designing responsive interactive applications by emotion-tracking and pattern-based dynamic user interface adaptation. In: Kurosu, M. (ed.) HCI 2016. LNCS, vol. 9733, pp. 28–36. Springer, Cham (2016). https://doi.org/10.1007/978-3-319-39513-5_3

16. Meixner, G., Calvary, G., Coutaz, J.: Introduction to model-based user interfaces. W3C Working Group Note, 07 January 2014. http://www.w3.org/TR/mbui-intero/. Accessed 27 May 2015

17. Melchior, J., Vanderdonckt, J., Van Roy, P.: A model-based approach for distributed user interfaces. In: Proceedings of the EICS 2011, pp. 11–20. ACM (2011)

18. Mens, K., et al.: A taxonomy of context-aware software variability approaches. In: Proceedings of the MODULARITY Companion 2016, pp. 119–124. ACM (2016)

19. Mulder, M., Borst, C., van Paassen, M.M.: Designing for situation awareness – the world behind the glass. In: Proceedings of the CHIRA 2017, pp. 9–21. SCITEPRESS (2017)

20. Navalpakkam, V., Churchill, E.F.: Mouse-tracking: measuring and predicting users' experience of web-based content. In: Proceedings of the CHI 2012, Austin, Texas, USA, 5–10 May, pp. 2963–2972 (2012)

21. Paternò, F.: ConcurTaskTrees: An Engineered Approach to Model-Based Design of Interactive Systems. ISTI-C.N.R., Pisa (2001)

22. Picard, R.: Recognizing stress, engagement, and positive emotion. In: Proceedings IUI 2015, Atlanta, GA, USA, 29 March–1 April 2015, pp. 3–4 (2015)

23. Qu, F., Wang, S.-J., Yan, W.-J., Fu, X.: CAS(ME)^2: a database of spontaneous macro-expressions and micro-expressions. In: Kurosu, M. (ed.) HCI 2016. LNCS, vol. 9733, pp. 48–59. Springer, Cham (2016). https://doi.org/10.1007/978-3-319-39513-5_5

24. Schilit, B.N., Theimer, M.M.: Disseminating active map information to mobile hosts. IEEE Netw. 8(5), 22–32 (1994)

25. Schmidt, A.: Biosignals in Human-Computer Interaction. Interactions 23, 76–79 (2016)

26. Stein, A., et al.: Interpolation in the eXtended Classifier System: an architectural perspective. J. Syst. Arch. 75, 79–94 (2017)

27. Warshaw, J., et al.: Can an algorithm know the "real you"? Understanding people's reactions to hyper-personal analytics systems. In: Proceedings of the CHI 2015, pp. 797–806. ACM (2015)

28. Yigitbas, E., Sauer, S., Engels, G.: A model-based framework for multi-adaptive migratory user interfaces. In: Kurosu, M. (ed.) HCI 2015. LNCS, vol. 9170, pp. 563–572. Springer, Cham (2015). https://doi.org/10.1007/978-3-319-20916-6_52

Evolution of Game Controllers: Toward the Support of Gamers with Physical Disabilities

Dario Maggiorini[✉], Marco Granato, Laura Anna Ripamonti,
Matteo Marras, and Davide Gadia

University of Milan, 20135 Milan, Italy
{dariomaggiorini,marcogranato,lauraripamonti,
davidegadia}@unimi.it, matteomarras@studenti.unimi.it

Abstract. Video games, as an entertaining media, dates back to the '50s and their hardware device underwent a long evolution starting from hand-made devices such as the "cathode-ray tube amusement device" up to the modern mass-produced consoles. This evolution has, of course, been accompanied by increasingly specialized interaction mechanisms. As of today, interaction with games is usually performed through industry-standard devices. These devices can be either general purpose (e.g., mouse and keyboard) or specific for gaming (e.g., a gamepad). Unfortunately, for marketing reasons, gaming interaction devices are not usually designed taking into consideration the requirements of gamers with physical disabilities. In this paper, we will offer a review of the evolution of gaming control devices with a specific attention to their use by players with physical disabilities in the upper limbs. After discussing the functionalities introduced by controllers designed for disabled players we will also propose an innovative game controller device. The proposed game controller is built around a touch screen interface which can be configured based on the user needs and will be accessible by gamers which are missing fingers or are lacking control in hands movement.

Keywords: Video game · Gaming devices · Input device · Game controller · Physical disability

1 Introduction

Video games, as an entertaining media, appeared around 1950. Since then, we have been able to observe their constant evolution in both hardware and interaction capabilities. Today, the role of video games in our lives is changing: they are now regarded as viable digital artifacts to deliver interactive stories, teach new skills (*edugames*), perform physical exercise (*exergames*), and much more. While the processing power, storage capabilities, and connectivity of gaming devices made huge leaps forward, the hardware apparatuses that let users interact with a game (namely *gaming controllers*, or just *controllers*) had a somewhat slower momentum focusing mainly on ergonomics and converging on – sometime legacy – industry standards. Modern controllers range from general purpose tools, inherited from office automation activities (e.g., mouse and

© Springer Nature Switzerland AG 2019
A. Holzinger et al. (Eds.): CHIRA 2017, CCIS 654, pp. 66–89, 2019.
https://doi.org/10.1007/978-3-030-32965-5_4

keyboard), to gaming specific tools (e.g., gamepads). As it is easy to observe, controllers evolved with limited consideration for gamers with physical disabilities.

A physical disability is defined as a limitation on an individual's physical functioning. This limitation may regard mobility, dexterity or stamina. A gamer suffering from mobility or dexterity limitations may experience issues in interacting with a video game. As an example, the player may not be able to provide specific inputs (or combinations of them) due to inability to press multiple buttons at once or move a finger between two positions in a timely manner. These limitations can make the gaming experience unbalanced at least, if not even completely frustrating [4, 29] for the gamer. As an example, it is almost impossible for a player missing the left hand to effectively use a standard modern gamepad. A keyboard is a more viable solution but, nonetheless, it might put a serious disadvantage on the player. To understand the extent of this phenomenon, just think that many devices in the past had limited consideration even for left-handed players; this can be observed e.g., in the *Nintendo Power Glove* released in 1989. The Nintendo Power Glove is a device designed for the Nintendo Entertainment System (NES). The user must wear the Power Glove on the right hand where tilt sensors and NES controller buttons are located. As a result, all gaming activity must be performed with the right hand while the buttons must be operated with the left one. As a matter of fact, this is putting a disadvantage on left-handed players.

Nevertheless, in recent years, a number of controllers have been designed for gamers with physical disabilities. These controllers are usually variations of industry standards where innovation is aiming to make standard retail games accessible to disabled players. As a result, an attribute shared by many of these controllers is that they try to make available all standard action in a simplified way rather than actually introducing new interaction models.

In this paper, we tackle on the problem of understanding the evolution of game controllers with respect to the usability by players with physical disabilities. In particular, we focus our study on controllers for players with disabilities in the upper limbs; i.e., players that are missing – or have difficulties using – a hand, or part of it. The innovations introduced by existing controllers are analyzed in order to design and propose a novel gamepad which is accessible to gamers with physical disabilities.

The remainder of this paper is organized as follows: in Sect. 2 we analyze the evolution of mainstream game controllers discussing their accessibility for disabled gamers, while Sect. 3 covers existing scientific literature addressing the problem. Current commercial and academic solutions to support physically impaired gamers are presented in Sect. 4. Section 5 describes our innovative solution: the One-Hand Controller, presenting its hardware, software, and interface architectures. Section 6 concludes the paper and outlines possible future research.

2 Evolution of Gaming Controller Devices

As already mentioned in the introduction, game equipment dates back to the early '50s with the invention of the *Cathode-ray tube amusement device* (1947). In this device, the player was supposed to use knobs in order to control the trajectory of a CRT beam spot. Unfortunately, the Cathode-ray tube amusement device was patented but never

Fig. 1. Tennis for Two reconstruction on a DuMont Lab Oscilloscope Type 304-A.

manufactured or marketed. Other two cases can be mentioned after 1947: *Nimrod* (1951) and *OXO* (1952). The Nimrod was a custom-built computer designed to play the game of *Nim* using a lightbulbs matrix, while OXO was obtained from a repurposed Electronic Delay Storage Automatic Calculator (EDSAC) computer to simulate a game of Noughts and Crosses (usually referenced as Tic-Tac-Toe) on a CRT. Nevertheless, the title of "first video game" is credited to *Tennis for Two* (1958) by Willy Higinbotham at the Brookhaven National Lab. In Tennis for Two an oscilloscope was used to display a tennis court viewed from the side; players adjusted the angle of their shots with a knob and hit the ball over the net by pressing a button. A reconstruction of Tennis for Two oscilloscope display is proposed in Fig. 1. Anyway, the most important thing for us is that Tennis for Two is reportedly the first gaming equipment using an actual game controller. This game controller, obtained from an aluminum box, was functional but absolutely not comfortable to human hands. A reconstruction of the original controller used by Higinbotham is depicted in Fig. 2. The second game equipped with controllers was *Spacewar!* (1962). The controllers in Spacewar! were very similar to those in Tennis for Two as form factor but used two double switches rather than a knob. An early design of this controllers is reported in Fig. 3. One important factor here is that, while Tennis for Two (using an oscilloscope) had a requirement for external input devices, Spacewar! ran on a DEC–PDP–1 and could use the console's single toggle switches. Nevertheless, the developers declared that native controls were not adequate for a game [11] and specific external controllers have been designed. This is reportedly the very first example of a game causing the development of a controller; as also discussed in [5].

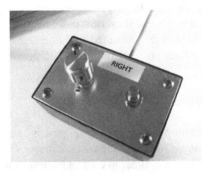

Fig. 2. Reconstruction of Tennis for Two controller.

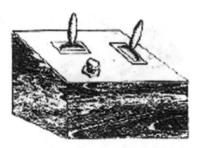

Fig. 3. Spacewar! controller design. Source: Creative Computing Magazine, August 1981.

Anyway, it goes without saying that sharp edged metal boxes were everything but ergonomic to use, let alone that disabled players where not considered at all. Knobs are impossible to manage without a decent finger grip and a push button alone was not a convenient way to play.

We have to wait until the beginning of the '70s to see the appearance of the first coin-operated (or coin-op) machines and gaming consoles. Coin-ops, such as *Galaxy Game* (1971), *Computer Space* (1971), and *Pong* (1972) were intended for public use and adopted controls bolted in the metal frame while gaming consoles like the *Magnavox Odyssey* (1972) have been marketed for home entertainment and used detachable controllers. Nevertheless, in the majority of the cases, the interaction model was still bound to a rotary wheel and one or two buttons. At this stage, controllers have been rebaptized *paddles* and improved in form factor. Actually, the form factor has been improved only for non-disabled gamers since paddles need to be held in one hand while operated with the other. The impossibility, in the majority of cases, to use a stable surface as a support further reduced accessibility for disabled players.

In the late '70s, with the second consoles generation, gaming controllers evolved into many shapes with different functionalities. Of those shapes, two are still mainstream today: the joystick and the gamepad. A joystick is an input device based on the design of an aircraft's control system and has been widely associated to Atari's consoles. The joystick proved to be the first truly generic control device fitting a huge number of games. Moreover, its operation proved to be possible also by gamers with – sometimes severe – limitations in the upper limbs. As a matter of fact, these same devices are also used to operate assistive medical devices such as motorized wheelchairs. The gamepad, on the other hand, was also introduced by Atari but it has been more largely associated to Nintendo's consoles. The first form of gamepad (also called joypad) featured a cross-shaped *D–Pad* button to move in four directions and two buttons for interaction; see e.g., Figure 4. While the joypad proved to be superior to the joystick thanks to smaller movement required to play, its use was still unfriendly to gamers with physical disabilities in the hands and, from their usability standpoint, a step back from the joystick.

After the introduction of joystick and joypad, many other gaming controllers have been proposed. For sake of clarity, and to keep our study focused, in the remainder of this section we will concentrate on gaming controllers to be operated using hands and with a reasonably high market/adoption relevance.

Fig. 4. The first gamepad from Nintendo (the joypad).

The following evolution of game controllers has been triggered by the introduction of 3D games thanks to the increased processing power available in the fifth consoles generation (1993–1998): the D-Pad, due to its four-directions nature, proved to be inefficient in navigating a 3D environment. As a result, the joystick was merged back to contribute with an analog finely-tuned control. The first console performing this merge back has been the *Nintendo 64* (1996), whose controller can be seen in Fig. 5. While using a standard joystick was a feasible task for a disabled gamer, a thumb-sized one to be used in coordination with the D-Pad rolled back the situation to the previous generation of controllers. Mainstream controllers were, once again, extremely difficult to manage for players with disabilities in the upper limbs.

Fig. 5. The Nintendo 64 gamepad.

Gamepads evolution observed just two other major steps forward. Both these improvements took place during the sixth console generation (1993–1998) and consisted in the addition of analog buttons (not used by any modern game actually) and the haptic feedback. Haptic feedback, in particular, is of little interest in the current discussion because it provides an output to the user instead of collecting inputs. As a result, gamepads changed in shape for a more favorable hold (for a non-disabled player) but are keeping today the same functionalities established with the Nintendo 64. A modern gamepad from Microsoft can be seen in Fig. 6.

Fig. 6. Microsoft Xbox One controller.

Despite the fact that gamepads did not change much over time, other kinds of controllers showed up in recent years proposing completely innovative interaction models: *motion control* and *computer vision interactivity*.

Motion control has been adopted by both the *Nintendo Wii* and the *Sony Playstation 3* consoles. While the *Sony Move* failed to be a commercial breakthrough due to limited support in mainstream games, the Nintendo *Wii Remote* and *Nunchuck* (Fig. 7) proved to be a real gamechanger in the interaction scenario. With the Wii Remote, D-Pad and thumbstick are separated in two controllers linked by a wire and a player can interact with the game by waggling each controller separately. Despite its lack of precision in registering movements, the Wii Remote become extremely popular among players, also because D-Pad and thumbstick, albeit available, did not any longer represent a major way of interaction. This acceptance has been extended to the point to exploit the controller for actual medical rehabilitation programs [10, 30]. Another interesting controller for the Nintendo Wii worth mentioning – despite not being operated with hands – is the *Wii Balance Board*. The Wii Balance Board used pressure sensors to monitor player's center of balance and weight and was also exploited in a number of rehabilitation programs [2, 18]. Unfortunately, the Wii Balance Board has not met a huge commercial success. Going back to the Wii Remote, it proved to be very useful to a number of disabled gamers: even when their finger control was limited this controller provided a very enjoyable experience. The same interaction model proposed by the Wii Remote has been kept by Nintendo up to the last console generation, on the *Nintendo Switch*. The Nintendo Switch features two detachable controllers called *Joy–Cons* which can be used in a similar way as the Wii Remote and Nunchuck. Despite this, Joy–Cons are smaller than their predecessors and current games require a more intensive use of buttons and thumbsticks, making them less attractive for a player with difficulties in using her hands.

Fig. 7. Wii Remote and Nunchuck.

Computer vision interactivity uses computer vision technology to analyze images of the player's movements and translate it into movement in the game. This has been attempted initially by Sony with the *EyeToy* device (2003) (Fig. 8 on the left) on the Playstation 2 and then relaunched by Microsoft with the *Kinect* (2010) (Fig. 8 on the right), which proved to be a huge commercial success. Like the Wii Remote, the Kinect has also been used in a relevant number of rehabilitation projects; see e.g., [6, 21, 22]. Kinect proved to be a really convenient and accessible device for gamers with disabilities. Nevertheless, it is worth mentioning that this convenience is limited to players suffering from reduced control. The body tracking technology is not currently able to cope with missing body parts and the presence of assistive devices such as wheelchairs. Moreover, we must also point out that limitation in movement (e.g., due to poor control of the lower limbs) and sensibility to physical exertion may put a severe limit to the gameplay.

A device similar in concept to the Kinect but specialized in short range hand tracking is the *Leap Motion Controller* (2013). The Leap Motion Controller uses infrareds to track finger positions. Unfortunately, this device assumes all fingers are in place when tracking and is not useful for gamers missing one or more.

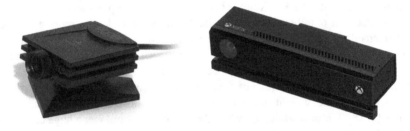

Fig. 8. Computer vision devices: Sony EyeToy (left) and Microsoft Kinect (right).

To close our historical analysis, we must also mention the most used gaming devices of all times: keyboard and mouse. Keyboard and mouse are not used on consoled but get normally adopted by PC gamers. Differently from their consoles' counterpart, these two input devices, probably due to their general–purpose nature, did not change much over the years. Today, it is possible to find many keyboards and mice on the market tailored for users with disabilities. Unfortunately, to the best of our knowledge, none of them are designed with gaming activities in mind. Usually, the addressed impairments are relative to not being able to see or hit the keys correctly when typing while typists with reduced movements can benefit from alternate physical layouts. Usually, a disabled player on PC is inclined to augment her setup with additional devices (e.g., pedals), use software aids (e.g., commands triggered by vocal patterns), or even create her own custom devices.

3 Related Work

Moving now to a more scientific ground, we can observe that in recent literature there is a vivid interest in game accessibility [28, 33, 34]. On this ground, the Independent Game Developers Association (IGDA) published already in 2004 a set of guidelines for gaming accessibility [16]. Unfortunately, these guidelines focused mainly on visual impairments, leaving out gamers suffering from physical limitation due to reduced mobility or missing limbs. The aforementioned guidelines have been updated by [24] in 2006, but their general goal was, unfortunately, not extended. Other interesting sources for accessibility guidelines, created as a collaborative effort with the academia, are represented by the Game Accessibility Guidelines website [9] and the AbleGamers Foundation's Game Accessibility Guidelines [3].

The scientific community is contributing to this topic by proposing innovative devices for disabled gamers with a higher accessibility when compared to ones available on the mass market.

To address the introduction of new devices, the research is mainly focused on making standard controllers available to impaired people through physical adaptation and integration with additional sensors, such as in [7, 15]. Unfortunately, their approach seems to be a bit intrusive and cumbersome to setup for the average player due to the additional wiring and sensors unsupported by the console vendor. Nevertheless, these contributions proved to be an interesting solution to support some cognitive disabilities.

Other researchers are working to completely exclude the physical interaction with a controller. To remove the physical interaction, it is possible to adopt Brain–Computer Interface (BCI) [20] or electromyography (EMG) [17, 32] technologies. Application of these approaches can also be found in commercial products such as the *Epoc+* (2013) from Emotiv and the *Myo armband* (2015) from Thalmic Labs.

The combination of the approaches above, may result in using a sensor system in place of a controller like in the case of the VoodooIO Gaming Kit [31]. In the VoodooIO Gaming Kit, players are allowed to place physical inputs as they need on a conductive fabric.

Alongside new devices, there is also a demand for methodologies on how to integrate them in new or existing games. To this purpose, we are witnessing a significative effort to provide guidelines to increase accessibility through game design.

In [25], we can find a study about making classic games accessible to disabled gamers. In this work, a middleware between the game and the I/O subsystem has been created using a descriptive language. This result aims to demonstrate that – technically – any game can be made compatible with any kind of device. Unfortunately, this approach seems to be too invasive for the game core architecture because it requires the (assistive) I/O device to have a direct API access to the hosting game engine. This requirement translates to the development of a game engine specific to the device and, in turn, to the supported disability. Another contribution along the same line [12] led to the creation of a game that, with specific changes to game mechanic and logic, can be adapted to any kind of player's disability. A very specific contribution is presented in [14], where the design of fast-paced action-oriented games for children with cerebral palsy is discussed. In this paper, a participatory design process is used to prove the feasibility of the approach and provide a set of recommendations to achieve action-orientation and playability.

Research on advanced game controllers is also performed outside the scientific community to the purpose of creating commercial products. Unfortunately, none of those reached popularity and become mainstream. Nevertheless, they have all been (and some of them still are) marketed. In the next session we are going to address game controllers for disabled gamers which have been proposed as commercial products.

4   Commercial Devices Suitable for Players with Disabilities

To overcome their physical limitations, impaired players usually look for specific input devices. On the market, many devices have been proposed by gaming-oriented companies to improve (or make possible) gaming experience of physically disabled players.

Most probably, the first (and the best) commercial example of a controller to support disabilities is the *NES Hands Free Controller* (1989) by Nintendo. This controller was designed for gamers totally unable to move the hands and/or a significative part of their body. This device must be strapped to the chest and hooked to the neck of the player (Fig. 9). For movements, the gamer can use her chin to move a joystick while buttons are simulated by blowing in a small pipe.

Fig. 9. A Kid wearing the NES Hands Free Controller. Source: [26].

After the NES Hands Free Controller, we have to wait almost ten years to see the *ASCII Grip Controller* (1996) from Agetec. This controller was originally designed for the fifth generation of game consoles (1993–1998) and conceived to let gamers play using only one hand while merging all interaction under the control of 5 fingers (Fig. 10). The goal of the ASCII Grip Controller was to support disabled gamers by making available all inputs which are present on a standard controller with minimal effort and movement.

Fig. 10. ASCII Grip Controller. Source: oneswitch.org.uk.

A similar solution to the ASCII Grip is proposed by the *DragonPlus DuoCon* (2008), where all the controls of a standard gamepad are placed on a tabletop case and the player can rest her hand on top of an ergonomic support. Controls are located at the end of the palm-resting platform to avoid straining (see Fig. 11). As it can be easily observed in the picture, the intended platform this controller was the Sony Playstation 3 (seventh generation). The DragonPlus DuoCon was updated in 2010 and re-baptized *One-Handed Ergonomic Palm Game Controller*. While the concept and form factor were still the same, this second version further extended consoles compatibility up to Playstation 4 and Xbox One.

Fig. 11. DragonPlus DuoCon Controller. Source: oneswitch.org.uk.

A very interesting step forward to support one-handed gamers is also represented by the *eDimensional Access Controller* (2008). As we can see in Fig. 12, like the previous one, also this controller extends the concept of tabletop case but, differently from the DragonPlus DuoCon, it is providing a modular architecture. Controls are divided into independent units and each unit can be plugged in a socket of the main case. By deciding the position of each control unit, a disabled gamer can customize the controller based on her specific disability.

Alongside with the companies we mentioned in this section, we can observe the constant growth of other organizations focused on helping disabled players. Worth mentioning are *OneSwitch* and *AbleGamers*. OneSwich offers an updated and affordable market for enabling gaming solutions, not just controllers. AbleGamers is a nonprofit public charity aiming to improve the overall quality of life for those with disabilities through video games. They create tailored solutions for single users and perform R&D for assistive gaming devices.

Fig. 12. OHC concept design. Source: [8].

5 OHC: A Novel and Accessible Gamepad

Designing a game or a device to cope with all possible disabilities is very difficult, but not impossible, as discussed by [25]. As already mentioned in the introduction, in this manuscript we are going to focus on gamers suffering from mobility issues in the upper limbs. In particular, our research targets players which are missing one hand (or part of it) or have severe limitations in the mobility of their dominant hand.

Starting from the above considerations and taking inspiration from the analysis we performed in the previous three sections, our guidelines can be summarized as follows:

- an analog joystick-like control is a requirement;
- the controller should not be held in one hand, but must lay flat on a supporting surface;
- controls should be configurable in order to adapt to each disability;
- compatibility with standard USB Host-Computer Interface must be granted in order to cooperate with other commercial products.

Working with the above guidelines, we designed *OHC*: One-Hand Controller. OHC leverages on a mix of analog and digital inputs. Analog inputs are collected by means of a physical thumbstick while buttons are emulated using a touch interface. This touch interface is positioned flat on a supporting surface and the controls it represents can be customized by the player in layout, orientation, and size. We selected a touch interface because of three important advantages over current hardware solutions. First, it allows a flexible and fine-tuned re-configuration of gaming controls. Second, it might be feasible to substitute the touch surface with a tablet or smartphone already owned by the player, thus achieving a consistent cost reduction. Last, as an ongoing project, a touch interface allows fast prototyping of controls layouts and easy data collection about hand posture and touch patterns. A concept design of OHC can be seen in Fig. 13. As it can be observed, the device is intended to be completely symmetrical; this way it can be easily flipped to support both right- and left-handed players.

The OHC controller has already been introduced in [8], in the following subsections we are going to describe its updated hardware and software architectures and will propose a new set of experiments to evaluate user acceptance rate.

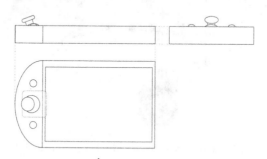

Fig. 13. eDimensional Access Controller. Source: oneswitch.org.uk.

5.1   OHC Hardware Architecture

OHC is built around a 7″ LCD multi-touch touchscreen equipped with an analog stick and two pushbuttons (provided for configuration purposes). The touchscreen supports up to five fingers at once and the analog stick is two-axis thumbstick. The controller hardware is managed by two interoperating microcontrollers: a Raspberry PI3 and an Arduino Leonardo. A scheme of the hardware setup is reported in Fig. 14.

The Raspberry PI microcontroller is in charge to drive the LCD touchscreen using the onboard Display Serial Interface (DSI). Using the DSI, the 7″ LCD can be driven at 25 frames per second. The Arduino Leonardo alone would not provide enough bandwidth to drive such a large display. Moreover, the Raspberry is also in charge to collect user inputs. These user inputs include both touches on the screen and the external thumbstick with pushbuttons. Unfortunately, there are no analog inputs on the Raspberry GPIO bus. Therefore, we were forced to use an Analog to Digital Converter (ADC) to convert the thumbstick position. To perform this conversion, we used an MCP3008, but any 10 bits converter supporting 5 V digital outputs can be used.

The Arduino Leonardo oversees managing the communication between OHC and the gaming PC. Leonardo has been used since it natively supports USB slave mode, and libraries to emulate mouse and keyboard are ready available. This way, the Raspberry PI can decode user input and use the Arduino to remap the result to legacy inputs for the game. Raspberry PI alone is not able to perform this task because it – as a system-on-chip computer – can only work as a USB Host.

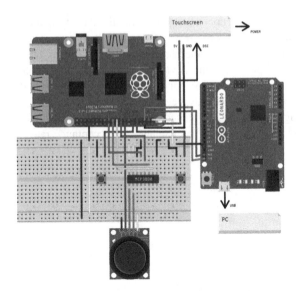

Fig. 14. OHC prototype board scheme. Source: [8].

A picture of the physical prototype we used for experiments can be seen in Fig. 15. Of course, for technical reasons, the physical prototype we built is much thicker than the final intended product. Nevertheless, we already planned the hardware disposition for a more refined – and thinner – version. This hardware disposition is visible in Fig. 16.

Fig. 15. OHC physical prototype.

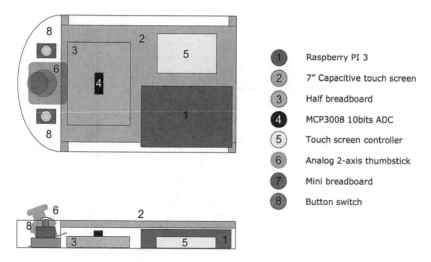

The following labels appear alongside the figure:

1. Raspberry PI 3
2. 7″ Capacitive touch screen
3. Half breadboard
4. MCP3008 10bits ADC
5. Touch screen controller
6. Analog 2-axis thumbstick
7. Mini breadboard
8. Button switch

Fig. 16. OHC Hardware disposition for a slimmer version.

5.2 Software Architecture

The software architecture is designed to favor the user experience. The main software goal is to virtualize a legacy controller starting from the touchscreen and thumbstick inputs. This task must also be performed with minimal delay.

When first turned on, the OHC software will perform a calibration. As a first step, the user is asked if she wants to (or can) use the buttons and thumbstick. Then, the user will be prompted to lay her hands on the touchscreen in a comfortable position. Starting from the detected touches, a default layout will be proposed, based on the number of available fingers. This layout will be aligned and stretched based on fingers' position. The layout can also be modified later for a better gaming experience.

The internal software supports multiple profiles. This allows several users to share a single device. Moreover, each user can store multiple layouts under her profile. As a result, each player can store a specific layout for each game, depending on personal taste and disability. For severe disabilities, or difficulties in coordinating fingers; macros are supported, and a single tap can be associated to multiple inputs (see also the next section).

The configuration menu can be accessed at any time from the controller itself. The controller touchscreen will provide menus to calibrate, configure controls, and save/load configuration without a requesting additional software on the PC/console (see Fig. 17 for a wireframe and Fig. 18 for a possible configuration sequence). This feature allows OHC to be more flexible and portable. Currently, there is no direct feedback provided to the game. This means that, during configuration, the game is not going to pause automatically, but it is possible to switch configuration/layout in any game while playing. Switching configuration automatically based on game status is not yet supported.

Finally, OHC can support gestures. Gestures are programmable combinations of command the user can associate to given touch patterns. When enabled, an area of the

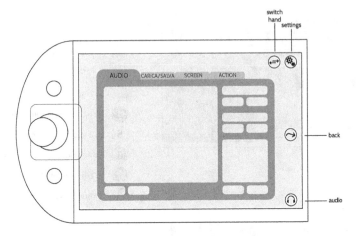

Fig. 17. OHC, Sample menu layout.

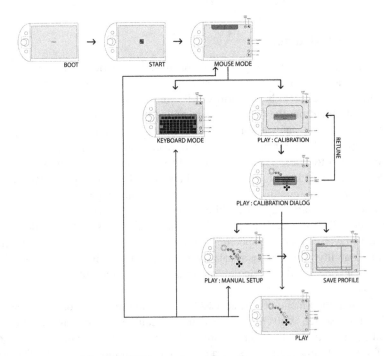

Fig. 18. OHC, sample configuration sequence.

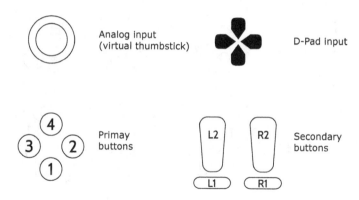

Fig. 19. Basic GUI Widgets. Source: [8].

touchscreen can be reserved to gesture recognition. Gestures will be detected by the Raspberry PI and translated into a sequence of keystrokes and movements. Currently, we support single, double, and triple touch, rotation, swipes, and two-fingers scrolling.

5.3   User Interaction

The Graphical User Interface is the most critical part of the OHC software. As a matter of fact, the GUI must be flexible enough to meet a huge range of user requirements. Moreover, it should also be easy to maintain and extend. For these reasons, we decided to leverage on the computational functionality of Raspberry PI and to implement it using Python and the Kivy framework [19]. Kivy supports the Tangible User Interface Objects (TUIO) paradigm to manage inputs from the touchscreen in a standard way.

The OHC GUI is implemented by composing visual widgets in a hierarchical way. Each widget is taking care of a specific kind of input. An overview of the implemented input widgets is reported in Fig. 19. When performing calibration, one or more widgets are assigned to each finger. Based on selected finger and feedback from the user, the widget will be rotated and stretched to maximize comfort and encompass any movement constraints the gamer may have. Fingers and hand discomfort are reduced by deforming the widget in a way to place each button very close to each finger landing point. Moreover, widgets position should help an easy switch between controls. Figure 20 shows default finger-based transformations applied to primary and secondary buttons.

Nevertheless, additional considerations are required to address missing or not usable fingers. To cope with every possible kind of disability, we designed specific default interfaces for each case. For every variant, a default widget-finger association is proposed, and the actual interface is the result of the deformation and the relocation of widgets basing on the information collected during calibration. Extra care must be devoted to understanding and detecting situations where widgets are too close to each other, hence becoming cumbersome, or, due to mobility constraints on one or more fingers, the widgets position may cause strain. When two widgets are too close the controls may not be effective, especially if the assigned finger has a reduced mobility.

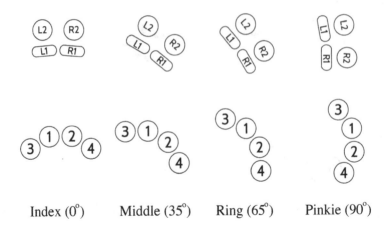

Index (0°)   Middle (35°)   Ring (65°)   Pinkie (90°)

Fig. 20. GUI buttons deformation based on finger. Source: [8].

Strain may be caused by physical conditions, considering that different fingers are sharing muscle and nerve connections. Default interfaces proposed to users having only four or three fingers are reported in Figs. 21 and 22, respectively. In the figures, the outlined areas indicate the working space for the touchscreen, while the large dark dots are fingers positions detected during calibration. The working area and the interface position are calculated starting from these dots.

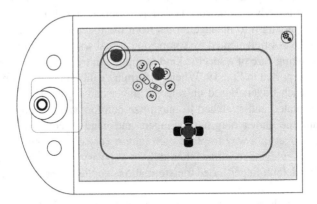

Fig. 21. Default interface for four fingers. Source: [8].

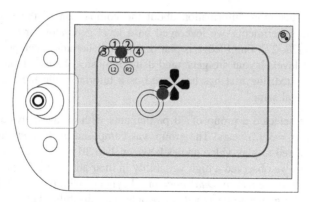

Fig. 22. Default interface for three fingers. Source: [8].

In the case of players having only one finger or missing the hand, the interface must provide a gesture area and should be customized by the user. In this case, we are proposing a dialpad instead of primary and secondary buttons. The result is shown in Fig. 23. This last case is where macros definition can be very useful. Macros can be used to associate a single gesture or a dialed number to complex movements or to a sequence of inputs on a standard controller.

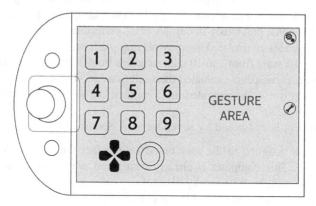

Fig. 23. Default interface for four one finger or no hand. Source: [8].

5.4   User Acceptance Tests

To evaluate the user experience while using OHC, we designed an experiment where the participants have been involved in a video games session. This experiment was designed with the single-blind paradigm: a sub-group of participants (test group) have to play the game first with OHC and then with a commercial gamepad while the other subgroups (control group) have to play the same game reversing the order of the controllers. A feedback form is filled out after each session. The use of both controllers is functional to get more information about the comparison of the two interaction models. For the experiments, we leveraged on a level generator for platform games: *Fun pledge 2.0* [23, 27]. Fun Pledge is platform level generator developed for research purposes where levels layout are generated using a musical base as input. Two levels have been generated; the first has been used as a tutorial while the second was the actual experimental setup.

Procedure. We selected a group of 20 participants with an age between 20 and 40 ($\mu = 25,15$ and $\sigma = 3.92$) years. The group was composed by 15 men and 5 women. Participants declared to play video games between 1 to 30 h per week ($\mu = 15.65$ and $\sigma = 9.53$). Albeit we observed a high variability in their adoption of input devices, the majority declared to use a *Sony Dualshock* or a keyboard with mouse. Only one of the participants used a gamepad designed for people with disability before. All the users used the right hand to interact with the OHC, even if one of them declared to be left handed. For the experiments, we accepted volunteers both with and without physical disabilities in the upper limbs. To people without any disability, we forced a temporary impairment by locking one hand and randomly tying zero, one or two fingers. As a result, the population was divided into three groups: people able to use all the fingers of one hand (25%), people able to use 4 fingers (35%), and people able to use three fingers (40%).

During the experiments, we arranged sessions with maximum two participants. To each participant, we explained the game mechanics and showed the initial part of the first level (the tutorial). The majority of users were not aware of the proposed game (80%) even if 50% of them claimed to have played similar games. The remaining 20% already tested the game previously in our lab while performing other research activities [13, 27]. Anyway, 55% of declared to enjoy playing platform games, and they rated the game difficulty on a scale from 1 to 10 with rankings from 2 to 8 ($\mu = 5$ and $\sigma = 1.65$). At the same time, participants evaluated themselves as good players in a range from 4 to 9 ($\mu = 7.05$ and $\sigma = 1.39$) and rated the complexity of game mechanics from 1 to 6 ($\mu = 3.2$ and $\sigma = 1.58$).

Each experiment is composed by seven steps as described below.

1. A computer is assigned to the user based on the fact she belongs to the test or control group. This computer is already configured with OHC or a commercial controller (we used an N30 Pro by 8Bitdo).
2. A first survey is proposed to profile the player.
3. The staff personnel help the user with gamepad setup and configuration and provide general information about the experiment. During this step, the tutorial level is used.
4. The second level is started, and the user must play by herself. This step will be over when the participant either (*i*) completes the level, or (*ii*) reaches the game over after 20 lives, or (*iii*) declares to have fully understood the interaction system with the game.
5. A second survey is proposed about the user experience.
6. If the user still needs to test a second controller, she will be moved to another computer and the protocol is restarted from step number 3.
7. Otherwise, a final survey is proposed to compare OHC with the commercial gamepad.

Experiment Outcome. As already pointed out, we evaluated the experiments by means of surveys. The results presented here are the average of the evaluations provided by the two groups (test and control). For sake of brevity, in the following, we will address the commercial controller simply as "N30". Moreover, all the scores reported below are related to a scale between 1 to 10.

According to the answers, neither of the controllers seem to cause relevant strain to the hand (3.1 for N30 and 3.7 for OHC). Unfortunately, even if users configured the buttons ahead of the game session, they reported a bad configuration for both controllers (4.4 for the test group and 5.8 for the control group). The test group also declared that the OHC was innovative as a device with a ratio of 6.8, whereas the control group evaluated the innovation for N30 equal to 4.4.

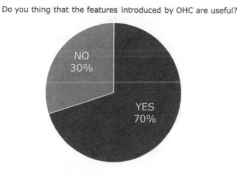

Fig. 24. Feedback about the usefulness of the features introduced by OHC.

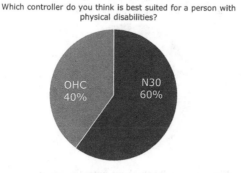

Fig. 25. Feedback about direct comparison between OHC and N30.

Specific questions about the design of OHC were also asked only at the test group. They claim that the device configuration was quite easy (6.2), albeit the software interface was not easy enough to understand (5.2). Furthermore, most of the participants evaluated the features introduced by OHC (e.g., the automatic button calibration using the fingertips) as useful (see Fig. 24). Despite this positive attitude, the general mood about how much OHC can help gamers with disabilities is negative, as reported in Fig. 25. Nevertheless, by means of unstructured interviews with the volunteers, it turned out that complaints were more directed toward the manufacturing status of the prototype. Among these complaints, we can mention the distance between thumbstick and display, the buttons size, and the case thickness. These, by the way, are already among the reasons why another hardware prototype is currently in the works (Fig. 16). To better understand this feedback, we can have a look at the answers we received to comparative questions. As a matter of fact, among the users who think that OHC is not suited for disabled gamers, 90% is also convinced that the new controller is very innovative (Fig. 26) and has a lot of potential in helping users with physical disabilities (Fig. 27).

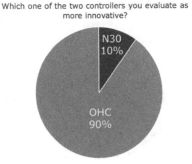

Fig. 26. Feedback about perceived innovation.

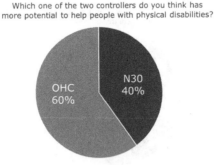

Fig. 27. Feedback about potential usefulness.

6   Conclusion and Future Work

In this paper, we discussed about the evolution of gaming control devices and how they try to cope with the requirement of disabled gamers. Our historical analysis seems to hint that mainstream commercial controllers can be exploited in some cases (e.g., a joystick or the Wii Remote Controller) but are not proceeding exactly in the needed direction. Nevertheless, many commercial controllers exist – even from first class manufacturer such as Nintendo – that are designed with specific disabilities in mind. By examining the evolution leading to modern controllers and existing solution we can come up with usability guidelines for controllers compatible with physical disabilities. In particular, we used these guidelines to propose OHC (One-Hand Controller). OHC is a gaming controller exploiting a touch surface for easy and fast layout adaptation and a thumbstick to allow exploration of 3D environments. A prototype has been built and tested via a single-blind set of experiments. Results are encouraging in term of potential usefulness but proved also that the first hardware prototype is not up to the task and need refactoring.

In the future, we are planning to finish refactoring the hardware of OHC to make it thinner and more comfortable to use. Moreover, we must arrange an additional round of experiments to test user acceptance with actually impaired gamers. Another possible improvement will be relative to the interface. The interface will be reworked from a graphical standpoint and a better widgets placement will be devised maybe considering the FFitts [sic] law [1].

References

1. Bi, X., Li, Y., Zhai, S.: FFitts law: modeling finger touch with fitts' law. In: Proceedings of the SIGCHI Conference on Human Factors in Computing Systems (CHI 2013), pp. 1363–1372. ACM (2013)
2. Baranyi, R., Willinger, R., Lederer, N., Grechenig, T., Schramm, W.: Chances for serious games in rehabilitation of stroke patients on the example of utilizing the Wii Fit Balance Board. In: IEEE 2nd International Conference on Serious Games and Applications for Health (SeGAH), pp. 1–7 (2013)
3. Barlet, C.M., Spohn, S.D.: Includification: A Practical Guite to Game Accessibility. The Able Gamers Foundation, Charles Town (2012). ISBN-13: 978-1479289356
4. Brown, M., Kehoe, A., Kirakowski, J., Pitt, I.: Beyond the gamepad: HCI and game controller design and evaluation. In: Bernhaupt, R. (ed.) Game User Experience Evaluation. HIS, pp. 263–285. Springer, Cham (2015). https://doi.org/10.1007/978-3-319-15985-0_12
5. Commings, A.H.: The evolution of game controllers and control schemes and their effect on their games. In: 17th Annual University of Southampton Multimedia Systems Conference, vol. 21 (2007)
6. D'Aquaro, N., Maggiorini, D., Mancuso, G., Ripamonti, L.A.: Videogames and elders: a new path in LCT? In: Duffy, V.G. (ed.) ICDHM 2011. LNCS, vol. 6777, pp. 245–254. Springer, Heidelberg (2011). https://doi.org/10.1007/978-3-642-21799-9_28
7. Fanucci, L., Iacopetti, F., Roncella, R.: A console interface for game accessibility to people with motor impairments. In: IEEE International Conference on Consumer Electronics-Berlin (ICCE-Berlin), pp. 206–210 (2011)
8. Gadia, D., Granato, M., Maggiorini, D., Marras, M., Ripamonti, L.A.: A touch-based configurable gamepad for gamers with physical disabilities. In: Proceedings of International Conference on Computer-Human Interaction Research and Application (CHIRA 2017), pp. 67–74 (2017)
9. Game Accessibility Guidelines web page. http://gameaccessibilityguidelines.com/. Accessed 12 Apr 2018

10. Gordon, C., Roopchand-Martin, S., Gregg, A.: Potential of the Nintendo Wii as a rehabilitation tool for children with cerebral palsy in a developing country: a pilot study. Physiotherapy (United Kingdom) **98**(3), 238–242 (2012)
11. Graetz, J.M.: The origin of spacewar. Creative Computing Issue 39 (1981)
12. Grammenos, D., Savidis, A., Stephanidis, C.: Designing universally accessible games. Comput. Entertain. **7**(1), 29 (2009)
13. Granato, M., Gadia, D., Maggiorini, D., Ripamonti, L.A.: Emotions detection through the analysis of physiological information during video games fruition. In: Dias, J., Santos, P.A., Veltkamp, R.C. (eds.) GALA 2017. LNCS, vol. 10653, pp. 197–207. Springer, Cham (2017). https://doi.org/10.1007/978-3-319-71940-5_18
14. Hernandez, H.A., Ye, Z., Graham, T.C., Fehlings, D., Switzer, L.: Designing action-based exergames for children with cerebral palsy. In: Proceedings of the SIGCHI Conference on Human Factors in Computing Systems (CHI), pp. 1261–1270 (2013)
15. Iacopetti, F., Fanucci, L., Roncella, R., Giusti, D., Scebba, A.: Game console controller interface for people with disability. In: International Conference on Complex, Intelligent and Software Intensive Systems, pp. 757–762 (2008)
16. IGDA Game Accessibility page. https://igda-gasig.org/about-game-accessibility/. Accessed 12 Apr 2018
17. Kawala-Janik, A., Podpora, M., Gardecki, A., Czuczwara, W., Baranowski, J., Bauer, W.: Game controller based on biomedical signals. In: Proceedings 20th International Conference on Methods and Models in Automation and Robotics (MMAR), pp. 934–939 (2015)
18. Kennedy, M.W., Schmiedeler, J.P., Crowell, C.R., Villano, M., Striegel, A.D., Kuitse, J.: Enhanced feedback in balance rehabilitation using the Nintendo Wii Balance Board. In: 13th International Conference on e-Health Networking, Applications and Services, pp. 162–168 (2011)
19. Kivy homepage. http://www.kivy.org/. Accessed 12 Apr 2018
20. Lopetegui, E., Zapirain, B.G., Mendez, A.: Tennis computer game with brain control using EEG signals. In: 16th International Conference on Computer Games (CGAMES), pp. 228–234 (2011)
21. Maggiorini, D., Ripamonti, L.A., Scambia, A.: Videogame technology to support seniors. In: Proceedings International ICST Conference on Simulation Tools and Techniques (SIMUTOOLS 2012) (2012)
22. Maggiorini, D., Ripamonti, L.A., Zanon, E.: Supporting seniors rehabilitation through videogame technology: a distributed approach. In: Proceedings International Workshop on Games and Software Engineering (GAS 2012) (2012)
23. Mazza, C., Ripamonti, L.A., Maggiorini, D., Gadia, D.: FUN PLEdGE 2.0: a FUNny Platformers LEvels GEnerator (Rhythm Based). In: Proceedings of the 12th Biannual Conference on Italian SIGCHI Chapter (CHItaly 2017), Article 22, 9 p. (2017)
24. Ossmann, R., Miesenberger, K.: Guidelines for the development of accessible computer games. In: Miesenberger, K., Klaus, J., Zagler, W.L., Karshmer, A.I. (eds.) ICCHP 2006. LNCS, vol. 4061, pp. 403–406. Springer, Heidelberg (2006). https://doi.org/10.1007/11788713_60
25. Ossmann, R., Miesenberger, K., Archambault, D.: A computer game designed for all. In: Miesenberger, K., Klaus, J., Zagler, W., Karshmer, A. (eds.) ICCHP 2008. LNCS, vol. 5105, pp. 585–592. Springer, Heidelberg (2008). https://doi.org/10.1007/978-3-540-70540-6_83
26. Plunkett, L.: The Disabled-Friendly NES Controller From The 1980's. On Kotaku (online) https://kotaku.com/5241760/. Accessed 12 Apr 2018
27. Ripamonti, L.A., Mannalà, M., Gadia, D., Maggiorini, D.: Procedural content generation for platformers: designing and testing FUN PLEdGE. Multimed. Tools Appl. **76**(4), 5001–5050 (2017)

28. Rowland, J.L., Malone, L.A., Fidopiastis, C.M., Padalabalanarayanan, S., Thirumalai, M., Rimmer, J.H.: Perspectives on active video gaming as a new frontier in accessible physical activity for youth with physical disabilities. Phys. Ther. **96**(4), 521–532 (2016)

29. Tollefsen, M., Lunde, M.: Entertaining software for young persons with disabilities. In: Miesenberger, K., Klaus, J., Zagler, W.L., Burger, D. (eds.) ICCHP 2004. LNCS, vol. 3118, pp. 240–247. Springer, Heidelberg (2004). https://doi.org/10.1007/978-3-540-27817-7_37

30. Tsekleves, E., Paraskevopoulos, I.T., Warland, A., Kilbride, C.: Development and preliminary evaluation of a novel low cost VR-based upper limb stroke rehabilitation platform using Wii technology. Disabil. Rehabil.: Assist. Technol. **11**(5), 413–422 (2016)

31. Villar, N., Gilleade, K.M., Ramdunyellis, D., Gellersen, H.: The VoodooIO gaming kit: a real-time adaptable gaming controller. Comput. Entertain. **5**(3), 16 (2007)

32. Watanabe, M., Yamamoto, T., Kambara, H., Koike, Y.: Evaluation of a game controller using human stiffness estimated from electromyogram. In: Proceedings of the 2010 Annual International Conference of the IEEE Engineering in Medicine and Biology, pp. 4626–4631 (2010)

33. Westin, T., Bierre, K., Gramenos, D., Hinn, M.: Advances in game accessibility from 2005 to 2010. In: Stephanidis, C. (ed.) UAHCI 2011. LNCS, vol. 6766, pp. 400–409. Springer, Heidelberg (2011). https://doi.org/10.1007/978-3-642-21663-3_43

34. Yuan, B., Folmer, E., Harris, F.C.: Game accessibility: a survey. Univ. Access Inf. Soc. **10**(1), 81–100 (2011)

The Role and Impact of Descriptive Theories in Creating Knowledge in Design Science

Antti Knutas[1]([✉]) [iD], Zohreh Pourzolfaghar[2], and Markus Helfert[2] [iD]

[1] Lero, The Irish Software Research Centre, Glasnevin, Dublin 9, Ireland
antti.knutas@lut.fi
[2] Dublin City University, Glasnevin, Dublin 9, Ireland

Abstract. In this paper, we clarify the role of descriptive knowledge in creating prescriptive knowledge with design science research. We demonstrate the connection by presenting an approach that utilizes kernel theories produced by the grounded theory research methodology in the creation of meta-level design science artefacts. These meta-level artefacts can be used to inform the design processes of situational artefacts, such as instantiations of software and services. We demonstrate and evaluate the approach further by using it to frame an ongoing research project that creates a meta-artefact to address issues in smart city service design.

Keywords: Design science · Kernel theory · Grounded theory · Descriptive knowledge · Prescriptive knowledge · Meta-artefact

1 Introduction

Design science research (DSR) at its core is the science of the artificial, involving scientifically rigorous creation of artefacts that have utility in an application domain and at the same contribute to the scientific body of knowledge [1, 2]. What is different in design science research from positivist research, is that a final outcome in design science research is *prescriptive knowledge* [3]. Design science research often begins with an important opportunity, challenging problem or a vision for the application domain [3, 4]. During the research process DSR produces both an artefact that addresses an issue in the application domain, and also prescriptive knowledge on how to change things [3]. In addition to instantiations of artefacts, design science processes can create higher level of artefacts such as design methods, principles, or theories. In natural and social sciences, a theory is likely to be seen as explaining and predicting a phenomenon [5]. Its nature is *descriptive*. Design science draws from a constructivist background and its main results are *prescriptive* [3]. Design theories as prescriptive knowledge are different from positivist, descriptive theories in the sense that a design theory does not only model, but also prescribes ways to act. Essentially a design theory gives prescriptions for design and action: it tells how to do something [3, 6].

Before a phenomenon or a situation can be changed, it is necessary to understand it in depth. Descriptive knowledge that explains a phenomenon is called justificatory knowledge [5] or a kernel theory [3]. The kernel theory that is used as a basis for artefact creation can also be tested and refined during the design science research

© Springer Nature Switzerland AG 2019
A. Holzinger et al. (Eds.): CHIRA 2017, CCIS 654, pp. 90–108, 2019.
https://doi.org/10.1007/978-3-030-32965-5_5

process [7]. Ostrowski and Helfert [8–11] presented a design science research framework which follows Goldkuhl and Lind's [12] division of design science research into a situational, empirical part (design practice) and abstract, design knowledge part (meta-design). The meta-design part is informed by descriptive theory, and the empirical part is in turn informed by the abstract design knowledge created in the meta-design process. In essence, the meta-design process creates a meta-artefact that guides situational design practice that occurs in a specific context [8, 12]. The meta-artefact provides more general design knowledge, is not situated in any specific context, and requires adaptation for a specific situation by the design science practitioner [12]. The approach by Ostrowski and Helfert uses business process modeling, engagement with practitioners, and literature reviews to create the justificatory knowledge as a basis for the design science research process and is most suitable for situations where it is possible to capture explicit organizational knowledge.

In this paper, we extend the original framework by Ostrowski et al. [8–11] and present an approach that uses grounded theory–based kernel theories as a basis for creating design science artefacts. The main novel contribution in this paper is using the approach to demonstrate and explain the bidirectional connection between the kernel theories and design science research processes. We also show how the evaluation part of the design process contributes to grounded kernel theory through constant comparison and grounding the kernel theory back to the data [13], which allows further development of the kernel theory when interacting with the application domain. Grounding, or connecting the research process to external knowledge, is essential in both grounded theory [14] and design science research [1, 12]. The main difference is that according to the principles of the grounded theory method, grounded theories are grounded back only to the empirical data [15]. By contrast, design science research methodology can include a more complex interplay of grounding processes between theories, artefacts, the body of scientific knowledge, and the application domain [12].

Compared to process modeling, grounded theory is more suitable for describing complex situations with human factors that are challenging to address with formal models [15]. Therefore, the approach presented in this paper is especially suited for socio-technical systems where the knowledge is tacit instead of formal, which is often the case in human societies and multi-stakeholder environments.

To demonstrate our approach for integrating grounded theory in creating abstract design knowledge we present an ongoing research case, originally introduced in [16, 17], on creating a taxonomy for informing smart city service design processes. This process was initiated by the observation that requirements engineering processes, as they exist in smart city service design today, need guidance. A taxonomy of concepts essential to service design would enable service developers to align requirements with the citizens' needs in a smart city context. However, how to ensure that the taxonomy responds to the needs of the application domain, is valid and is scientifically rigorous?

We summarize the research goals of this paper as follows.

1. Clarify the bidirectional connection between kernel theories and design science processes. This is accomplished by presenting an approach that utilizes grounded theory to generate kernel theories as an input for Ostrowski and Helfert's meta-level design science process [8–11].

2. Demonstrate the novel approach by presenting a case where a design science research process is used to create a meta-level artefact in the form of a taxonomy of smart city elements.

The rest of the paper is structured as follows. In Section two review the design science research approach and in Section three we review the grounded theory research method. In section four we present our approach to connect the generation of descriptive knowledge to design science processes. In Section five we evaluate the approach by using it to frame an ongoing research project. The paper ends with Section six, conclusion.

2 Design Science Research Approach

The overall research approach for this paper is design science [1], which is commonly used in the information system sciences to create artefacts in the form of instantiated systems or new design knowledge [3]. Hevner and Chatterjee [18, p. 5] define design science research as follows:

> "Design science research is a research paradigm in which a designer answers questions relevant to human problems via the creation of innovative artifacts, thereby contributing new knowledge to the body of scientific evidence. The designed artifacts are both useful and fundamental in understanding that problem."

From the above, Hevner and Chatterjee [18, p. 5] derive the first principle of DSR: "The fundamental principle of design science research is that knowledge and under-standing of a design problem and its solution are required in the building and appli-cation of an artefact." What essentially separates the design science research process from routine design practice is the creation of new knowledge [1]. If the design process is rigorous, it is based on existing theories and produces new scientific knowledge, then the process can be considered design science research.

Design science research is well applicable in situations where humans and software systems intersect [18], like information systems research. What makes information systems research unique is that it investigates the phenomenon where technological and social systems intersect [19] in the form of socio-technical systems, which requires a research methodology that takes both into account.

The concept of an artefact is at the core of the research science process. In a synthesis of the Sciences of the Artificial [20] and Developing a Discipline of the Design/Science/Research [21] by Hevner and Chatterjee [18], they broadly define artefacts, which are the end-goal of any design science research project, as follows: Construct (vocabulary and symbols), models (abstractions and representations), methods (algorithms and practices), instantiations (implemented and prototype sys-tems), and better design theories. Gregor and Hevner [3] further divide design science research outputs into three maturity levels, with level one being most situational and level three being most abstract. This progression also follows the produced research knowledge's maturity level, or how far has the contribution has advanced in terms of the characteristics of a well-developed body of knowledge [3]. This categorization is presented in Table 1.

Table 1. Design science research contribution types by Gregor and Hevner [3].

	Contribution type	Example artefact
More abstract, complete, and mature knowledge	Level 3. Well-developed design theory about embedded phenomena	Design theories (mid-range and grand theories)
	Level 2. Nascent design theory—knowledge as operational principles/architecture	Constructs, methods, models, design principles, technological rules
More specific, limited, and less mature knowledge	Level 1. Situated implementation of artefact	Instantiations (software products or implemented processes)

The seminal paper by Hevner et al. [1] on design science in information systems research does not present a model or process for performing design science research. However, a later paper [2] refines the concept further and identifies the existence of three design science cycles that are present in all design research projects. These cycles are the Relevance Cycle, which connects the contextual environment to the research science project, the Rigor Cycle, which connects the design activities to the knowledge base of scientific foundations, and the Design Cycle which iteratively connects the core activities of building a design artefact and research.

Hevner's three cycle view clarified the elements of design science research, but it still didn't provide systematic steps for conducting it. To provide a process model Peffers et al. [22] synthesized a design science research methodology from the evolving body of knowledge on design science. The process contains six activities, which are summarized as follows: Problem identification and motivation, defining the objects for a solution, design and development, demonstration, evaluation and communication.

2.1 Creating Meta-Level Artefacts

In this section, we describe the abstract design knowledge framework by Ostrowski and Helfert [8–11], which follows Goldkuhl and Lind's [12, 23] division of design science research into an empirical part (a design practice) and a theoretical part (meta-design). Their design knowledge framework presents a process for creating meta-artefacts, which consist of abstract design knowledge. These meta-artefacts in turn can be used in the creation of situational design knowledge, such as instantiations of IT systems. The different artefact types introduced by Hevner et al. [1, 3] are divided by Goldkuhl and Lind [12] into situational and abstract, instead of by the level of maturity. This alternative categorization is presented in Table 2.

Abstract meta-design artefacts can be used as (1) a preparatory activity before situational design is started, (2) a continual activity partially integrated with the design practice, or (3) a concluding theoretical activity summarizing, evaluating and abstracting results directed for target groups outside the studied design and use practices [12]. These types of meta-artefacts are general, abstract and apply to "unreal situations" [24, 25]. However, meta-design produces solid basis for design science activities to construct solutions for real environments, systems and people [9, 12].

Table 2. Design science research artefacts differentiated into abstract and situational [12].

Activity type and outcome	*From meta-design:* Abstract design knowledge	*From design practice:* Situational design knowledge and results
Constructs	Abstract concepts	Situational concepts (may be applied and adapted from abstract concepts)
Models	Generic models	Situational models
Methods	Guidelines for design practice	Parts of a situational system or process
Instantiations	(System abstraction with key properties)	IT systems (prototype or working system)

Ostrowski and Helfert [9] extended Peffers's design science research process [22] to include the split of design knowledge into abstract and situational [12], and the split of evaluation into naturalistic and artificial [25, 26]. The process created by Ostrowski and Helfert is presented in Fig. 1. They further divide the meta-artefact design process into three steps that interact with each other: Modelling, literature review and engagement scholarship [9, 10].

In the abstract design knowledge phase two levels of knowledge, literature and design experts, contribute to create reference models for design [10]. Literature review allows developing an initial scope and reviewing existing knowledge, and collaboration with practitioners allows ensuring problem relevancy and gaining current design knowledge. These two information sources are combined to a reference model, which allows modelling and evaluation of solutions [8, 10]. This model is then compared to existing body of knowledge as theoretical grounding in a rigor cycle, and to designers for the design practice phrase in a meta-relevance cycle [10].

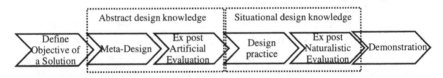

Fig. 1. The design science research method process [22] extended by Ostrowski and Helfert to include the meta-design step [9].

In Fig. 2 we extend Hevner's three cycle view [2] to include the split between abstract and situational knowledge according to ideas presented by Ostrowski and Helfert [9]. The original three cycle view included only the top half. In the extended view the top level contains the application environment and situational design. The lower level contains the creation of abstract design knowledge, which informs and guides the design of situational artefacts.

The lower half of the Fig. 2 presents how both design experts and the body knowledge contribute to the creation of new meta-artefact. Literature review allows developing an initial scope for the solution from existing knowledge. Collaboration with practitioners allows ensuring problem relevancy and benefits from their applied design knowledge. This model is then compared to existing body of knowledge in theoretical grounding in a rigor cycle, and back to the designers in the meta-relevance cycle.

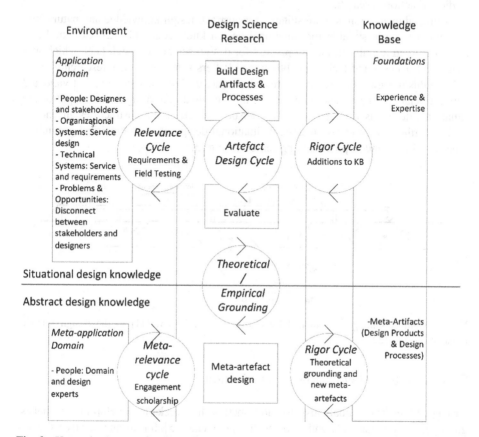

Fig. 2. Hevner's three cycle view [2] extended with the division to situational and abstract design knowledge [17].

The knowledge exchanges presented in Fig. 2 also form the three-part grounding process: Theoretical, empirical and internal grounding [12]. Theoretical and empirical grounding occurs between the meta-artefact and the artefact design cycle, and internal grounding occurs in both artefact design cycles.

2.2 Evaluating and Grounding Abstract Design Knowledge

As with all design science research, the validity of the artefact is judged by its utility [1]. The artefact resulting from meta-artefact design should be evaluated to establish its validity both before and after applying it to the artefact design cycle.

There are two levels of evaluation in design science research: artificial and naturalistic [25, 26]. Artificial evaluation is contrived or non-real in some manner and may consist of simulations, field experiments or lab experiments. Naturalistic evaluation is full evaluation of the situational artefact in its intended environment, the application domain. Naturalistic evaluation may consist of methods such as case studies, survey studies or action research.

Artificial evaluation is more suitable for abstract design knowledge and naturalistic evaluation is more suitable for situational design knowledge [11, 12]. Goldkuhl and Lind presented a multi-grounding process for design science research [12], which was used by Ostrowski and Helfert [11] to extend Peffers's design science research process [22]. In this design process, newly created abstract design knowledge is first validated with artificial evaluation and then used to inform situational design. The output of the situational design is validated with naturalistic evaluation and abstract design knowledge is further validated by successful situational design after an empirical grounding process. The extended process is presented in Fig. 3.

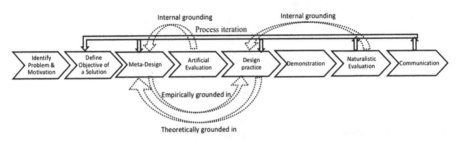

Fig. 3. Multi-grounding [12] applied by Ostrowski and Helfert [11] to the design science research process [22].

3   Grounded Theory Research Method

Grounded theory is a qualitative research method that seeks to develop theory that is grounded in systematically gathered and analyzed data [15]. It is a "an inductive, theory discovery methodology that allows the researcher to develop a theoretical account of the general features of a topic while simultaneously grounding the account in empirical observations or data" [27, p. 1]. Essentially, it can produce descriptive knowledge of novel situations or phenomena where no such knowledge yet exists. In information systems, grounded theory has been useful in developing context-based, process-oriented descriptions and explanations of information systems phenomena [15].

The objective of grounded theory is the discovery of a theoretically comprehensive explanation about phenomena, using techniques and analytical procedures that enable investigators to develop a theory that is significant, generalizable, reproducible and rigorous [28]. The aim of grounded theory is not only to describe a phenomenon, but also to provide an explanation of relevant conditions, how actors respond to the conditions and consequences of the actors' actions [15, 29]. For data analysis, it has a systematic set of procedures that support the development of theory that is inductively derived and continuously tested against empirical data through constant comparison [13]. The four principles of grounded theory research method have been summarized by Urquhart [15] as follows from the line of research performed Glaser and Strauss, first together [13] and then in divergent lines of research [30–32].

1. Main purpose of grounded theory is theory building.
2. Researchers should prevent prior knowledge of the field and preformulated hypotheses from hindering the emergence of ideas.
3. Analysis and conceptualization are engendered through the core process of *joint data collection* and *constant comparison*, where every slice of data is compared with all existing concepts and constructs. New knowledge from data is used to enrich an existing category, or to form a new category or relation.
4. "Slices of data," which can be of diverse types and from various sources, are selected in a process of theoretical sampling, where the researcher decides analytically the next source for sampling.

A key object in grounded theory is to aim for increasingly greater depth of analysis [13]. Urquhart et al. [15] have summarized three major steps in grounded theory research process following Glaser's approach to grounded theory [30], which are presented in Table 3.

Table 3. Three major phases of grounded theory research [15] with increasing depth of analysis.

Grounded theory research step	Summary
Open coding (description)	Describing conceptual constructs involved in the phenomenon and their properties
Selective coding (interpretation)	Defining and explaining the interactions between the conceptual constructs. Refining and generalizing. Understanding and explaining the area under investigation
Theoretical coding (formulating a theory)	Formulation of a descriptive theory. Aim is to create inferential and/or predictive statements about the phenomena. Achieved by defining relationships between individual interpretive constructs. E.g. associations, influences or causal

Just as in design science research, grounded theory has outputs that work towards increasingly abstract knowledge. Urquhart et al. [15] have defined three levels of theories by the level of abstraction: (1) narrow concepts, (2) substantive theories, and (3) formal theories. Substantive theories have been generated within a specific area of inquiry and are limited in scope. The highest level of abstraction is a "formal theory", which focuses on conceptual entities, such as organizational knowledge [31]. These levels are summarized in Table 4. One method to expand a grounded theory and contribute to the body of knowledge is to use theoretical generalization, which uses similar theories from the body of knowledge to expand the newly developed grounded theory [15].

Gregor [33] defines five types of theory in information systems research: analysis, explanation, prediction, explanation and prediction, and design and action. Urquhart et al. [15, p. 365] suggest that "grounded theory has the capability to generate theory that exists in all these categories because it contains the essential building blocks of any theory – constructs in the form of categories and relationships between those constructs in the form of theoretical coding." However, we propose that the grounded theory is most suited for the first four, as grounded theory is most adept at analyzing constructs and explaining their relationships. By contrast, according to Gregor and Hevner [3], most abstract knowledge and theory created by design science research are of the fifth type, design and action.

Table 4. Grounded theory output scopes [15].

Grounded theory scope	Description
Bounded context	Narrow "seed" concepts, based on limited fieldwork and anecdotal evidence
Substantive focus	Generated through a rigorous application of grounded theory procedures. A substantive theory extends its predictive and explanatory power to the specific set of phenomena from where it was developed
Formal concepts	A formal theory that spans a set or family of several substantive areas. Applies to many kinds of situations, systems and organizations. Rare in scientific literature

4 Creating Abstract Design Knowledge with Grounded Kernel Theories

In this section, we present how descriptive knowledge created by the grounded theory research method [13] can be used as a kernel theory for design science research processes. Grounded theory can produce knowledge useful to design science research because a design science researcher is dependent on the descriptive knowledge base for descriptive and propositional knowledge that informs the research [3]. *The better the situation and the phenomena involved are understood, the better it can be affected by the creation of novel artefacts.*

We establish a connection between a grounded theory-based kernel theory and a design science process by using the DSR theory development framework created by Kuechler and Vaishnavi [6] to extend the meta-artefact creation process [9–11]. Our novel contribution is presenting an approach that specifically uses grounded theory for descriptive knowledge and demonstrating how it can contribute to the creation of any design science artefact, not only design theories. This approach builds on Ostrowski and Helfert's framework [8–11], Goldkuhl and Lind's division of abstract and situational design knowledge [12], and artificial and naturalistic evaluation processes in design science [25, 26]. According to Gregor and Hevner [3, p. 343] "a design science research begins with an important opportunity, challenging problem, or insightful vision/conjecture for something innovative in the application environment." We propose that in order for the vision to be gained, the problem domain needs to be understood, and one method to understand the problem domain is to use grounded theory to generate an understanding of the phenomenon.

Our approach is most suited for situations where no previous descriptive understanding exists, or otherwise the researcher would obtain the required information from the existing body of knowledge. In Fig. 4 we present an overview of the approach. It begins by using grounded theory to generate an initial grounded theory of the application domain, which becomes the grounded kernel theory in the artefact design process. This knowledge helps in the creation of the research goals and predicting the artefact's impact. Then the research team either creates a meta-artefact or obtains it from the existing body of knowledge to inform their artefact design. Finally, the created situational artefact solves an issue in the application domain. The application of the artefact also contributes feedback to the grounded kernel theory. As the application domain changes after introducing the artefact, the descriptive theory can be evaluated and improved in regard to the explanations and predictions it provides.

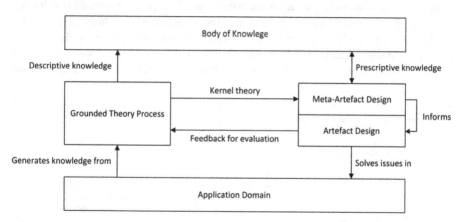

Fig. 4. The cycle of knowledge contributions between the descriptive grounded theory and design science knowledge processes.

The exchange between descriptive and prescriptive, and abstract and situational contains feedback loops at every step, all of which were not detailed in Fig. 4 for reasons of clarity. The artefact design process contributes abstract prescriptive knowledge to the body of knowledge, and the naturalistic evaluation that occurs in deploying the situational artefact to the application domain enables the validation of the meta-artefact following the multi-grounding principles [12]. These exchanges of information are detailed in the more detailed model presented in the next subsection.

4.1 An Approach for Creating Abstract Design Knowledge with Grounded Kernel Theories

Ostrowski's framework for creating abstract design knowledge as meta-artefacts for information systems recommends three steps for creating models for information systems: (1) Literature review, (2) collaboration with practitioners in engagement scholarship [34], and (3) then creating a solution model using one of the business modelling languages [8–10].

In this section, we present an approach that uses grounded theory [13] as defined by Urquhart et al. [15, 35] for information systems research to generate a kernel theory for a design science process. The grounded theory-based kernel theory enables understanding a phenomenon and creating abstract design knowledge based on that understanding. In our design, we follow the line of research that discusses and develops approaches for using descriptive knowledge as a basis for design theories [3, 5, 7, 23, 28, 36, 37]. This approach for creating kernel theories is valuable for situations that involve complex human factors, or for situations where there is an incomplete understanding of the phenomenon, the involved actors, and their relationships. The grounded theory method enables in-depth understanding of the problem by creating a situational, descriptive kernel theory that in turn informs the creation of the prescriptive artefact. As design science research problems are often complex problems that involve socio-technical systems [3] in complex interactions among subcomponents of the problem and its solution [1], in-depth understanding of the problem domain is valuable.

In Fig. 5 we present a model of the entire process as synthesized from guidelines by Urquhart et al. [15, 35] for grounded theory in information systems research, a line of research on design theories [3, 5, 7, 12, 23, 36], and the design science process by Ostrowski and Helfert [8–11]. Our novel contribution to this model is an approach for

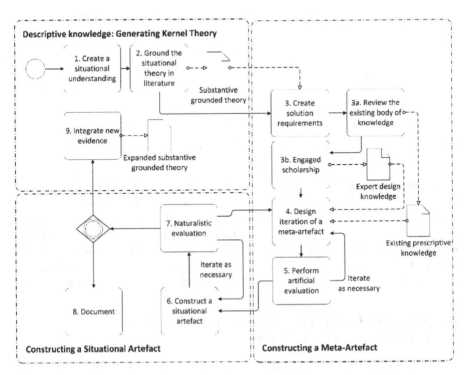

Fig. 5. Connecting grounded theory to design science research process with a kernel theory.

using a kernel theory generated by the grounded theory method as an input in a design science process. Additionally, we present how the design science process can contribute back to the further development of grounded theory.

Grounding is essential in our approach to knowledge contributions. The grounded theory is grounded to the empirical data from the phenomenon (internal to step 1). Meta-design (step 4) is theoretically grounded to the kernel theory and empirically grounded in the naturalistic evaluation process (step 7). Eventually the situational design (step 6) produces enough evidence during naturalistic evaluation (step 7) to contribute new evidence to develop the grounded theory further (step 9).

We detail the steps presented in the model of Fig. 5 in Table 5.

Table 5. Steps for creating a kernel theory and using it to contribute to design science research.

Process step	Activities	Outputs
1. Create a situational understanding	Using the three main steps of grounded theory to generate a kernel theory that explains the phenomenon, its constructs and their relationships	A substantive grounded theory not yet connected to literature
2. Ground the situational theory in literature	Comparing the grounded theory with the descriptive body of knowledge and using existing knowledge to scale it up. (Grounded theory does not mandate a literature review, but it can be used for theoretical integration after the initial research [15])	Substantive grounded theory that can be used as a kernel theory
3. Create solution requirements	Developing initial requirements for a solution based on an understanding of the situation with the help of the kernel theory	Research goals for the design science research process
3a. Review the existing body of knowledge	Finding existing prescriptive knowledge that can assist in creating a solution	Existing prescriptive knowledge and solutions from the body of knowledge
3b. Engaged scholarship	Engaging design experts in evaluating solutions and exploring the design space	Expert design knowledge
4. Design iteration of a meta-artefact	Designing a meta-artefact to inform the creation of situational artefacts	Meta-artefact
5. Perform artificial evaluation	Evaluating the meta-artefact e.g. with simulations, lab experiments or field experiments	Evaluation results for the meta-artefact
6. Construct a situational artefact	Creating an artefact that addresses the issue in the situation in the application domain	Situational artefact
7. Naturalistic evaluation	Empirical evaluation of the situational artefact in the application domain	Evaluation results for the situational artefact
8. Document	Documenting and communicating the results	Prescriptive knowledge contribution to the body of knowledge
9. Integrate new evidence	Developing the grounded theory further with new data on the phenomenon	Expanded substantive grounded theory

4.2 Connecting Grounded Theory to Design Science Research Process as Kernel Theory

The main tenet of the grounded theory method is developing new theory. However, common outputs in grounded theory research are substantive, explanatory theories instead of the grand theories which first come to mind when the word "theory" is mentioned. Design theories also have been called theories of the middle range [3], or by Merton [38, p. 39] "theories that lie between the minor and necessary working hypotheses that evolve in abundance during day-to-day research and the all-inclusive systematic efforts to develop a unified theory that will explain all the observed uniformities of social behavior, social organization, and social change." The descriptive middle-range theories created by the grounded theory are similar in scope to prescriptive design theories and can inform the creation of new abstract design knowledge.

A *kernel theory* is defined by Walls et al. [39] as theories from natural sciences, social sciences or mathematics that are encompassed in design theory. Gregor and Jones [5] further define kernel theory to any descriptive theory that informs artefact construction, and Gregor and Hevner [3] present that a mature body of design knowledge should include a kernel theory. By contrast, we define *justificatory knowledge* to include any descriptive knowledge that informs design research [3]. Depending on how far the grounded theory research process advances towards abstract knowledge generation, it can create either. Bounded context or substantive focus combined selective coding can produce justificatory knowledge. Theoretical coding with substantive focus can generate grounded theories to be used as kernel theories. We relate these levels of grounded theory output scopes to inputs in design science research in Table 6. At all levels the knowledge created by grounded theory research can inform design science research processes *by enabling a better understanding of the situation and the phenomena.*

Table 6. Relating grounded theory outputs to design science research process inputs.

Grounded theory research step	Grounded theory output scope	Use in design science research
Selective coding	Bounded context or substantive focus	Justificatory knowledge
Theoretical coding	Substantive focus or formal concepts	Kernel theory

Kuechler and Vaishnavi [7] state that kernel theories can *inform* design science research and additionally design science research can in turn *be refined and developed* by the design science research process. They present an approach based on Venable [26] and Goldkuhl [23], where new empirical evidence created by naturalistic artefact evaluation allows evaluating the kernel theory. The new evidence as a form of descriptive knowledge can be confirmed by the kernel theory or lead to revision of the kernel theory [7]. A grounded theory research process can benefit from new empirical evidence created in a design science process, because constant comparison and evaluation of the theory against the data is one of the central principles in grounded theory.

5   Evaluating the Approach for Creating Abstract Design Knowledge with Grounded Kernel Theories

In this section, we evaluate our approach by using it to frame an existing design science research case. From a certain perspective, our approach can be considered a design science meta-artefact as well because it can be used to inform situational design, or actual research in this case. As a meta-artefact the most suitable evaluation method for our approach is artificial evaluation. We begin by summarizing an ongoing research case by Pourzolfaghar et al. to create meta-design artefacts to inform the creation of services in a smart city context. We begin with a brief definition of smart cities, how the ongoing research relates to smart services and the summarize the project's research goals. Then in the next subsection we relate their research design to the design science research approach presented in Sects. 4 and 4.1 and present the evaluation results.

The definition for smart cities that Pourzolfaghar et al. use is that smart cities are innovative cities, which use ICT to improve quality of life for citizens [40–42]. According to Ferguson [43] services are the enablers in the digital cities and therefore, responsible to improve the citizens' quality of life. In other words, the services in the smart cities need to respond to the needs of the citizens. In this regard, Pourzolfaghar and Helfert [16] have defined the term 'smart service' for the services which meet the smart cities quality factors and respond to the smart cities stakeholders' concerns.

Pourzolfaghar et al. began their research project by identifying shortcomings in how currently smart city services were designed. This first step involved the researchers performing a series of interviews and producing descriptive knowledge about the current status of service design. From the discovery phase they proceeded to addressing the issue by developing a taxonomy for smart service elements which can be used to inform the design of smart services. This taxonomy is essentially a meta-artefact because it gives prescriptive knowledge towards creation of situational smart service artefacts, such as requirements or service instantiations.

5.1   Framing the Research Case as a Process to Create a Meta-Artefact

In this section, we frame the ongoing design science research project on smart city services using the approach presented in Sects. 4 and 4.1. The Table 7 presents the project steps using a similar structure we used to introduce our approach in Table 5. Steps 1 to 4 of the research project have been completed at the time of publication, with step 5 ongoing. Steps 6 to 9 are planned as future work.

Table 7. Framing the design science project by Pourzolfaghar et al. with our design science approach.

Process step	Activities	Outputs
1. Create a situational understanding	Using a grounded theory -inspired coding process to analyse the interviews on smart city service design	Initial justificatory knowledge
2. Ground the situational theory in literature	Performing a literature review on the body of knowledge on smart cities	Kernel theory at bounded context level
3. Create solution requirements	Developing research goals for improving smart city service design processes	Research goal: Developing a taxonomy to inform smart service design processes
3a. Review the existing body of knowledge	Finding existing prescriptive knowledge that can assist in creating a solution for service design	Selecting the TOGAF architecture vision development template [44]
3b. Engaged scholarship	Engaging design experts at workshops and conferences	Expert design knowledge
4. Design iteration of a meta-artefact	Designing first iteration of the taxonomy	First version of the taxonomy
5. Perform artificial evaluation	Presenting the taxonomy to practitioners and stakeholders and gaining feedback for the second iteration	Initial, non-systematic evaluation for the meta-artefact
6. Construct a situational artefact	Using the taxonomy to inform the creation of artefacts related to smart services	Smart service requirements and instantiations
7. Naturalistic evaluation	Empirical evaluation of the situational artefact in a smart city context	Evaluation results for the situational artefact
8. Document	Documenting and communicating the results to practitioners, the application domain, and the body of knowledge	Prescriptive knowledge contribution to the stakeholders and the body of knowledge
9. Integrate new evidence	Developing the kernel theory further with new data on the phenomenon	Expanded descriptive knowledge

5.2 Artificial Evaluation of the Approach for Creating Abstract Design Knowledge with Grounded Kernel Theories

In this section, we evaluate the utility of our approach to connect kernel theories to design science research processes. We performed the evaluation by demonstrating the approach to the practitioners and then simulated the research project with the research group by using the steps presented in the previous subsection (Table 7). Evaluation data was gathered from the research group with interviews. This is an initial form of artificial evaluation [26], which should establish a preliminary utility of our approach [25], and thus first steps towards validity [1].

The members of the research group were interviewed first individually and then as a group. The research group agreed that the plan is beneficial, and the approach could inform their meta-artefact design process. While not a full proof of the framework's validity, it can be considered a promising initial evaluation and suggests that the evaluation should proceed with further, empirical testing. The interview-based evaluation found the following benefits from the proposed approach.

- The design process involves complex problems in sociotechnical systems within multi-stakeholder environments. In this case, the proposed approach for gaining descriptive knowledge with grounded theory would be suitable.
- The approach brought knowledge exchanges into clearer focus for the research group and helped them to position the research project's descriptive knowledge contributions.
- The approach helped the research group to evaluate the role of justificatory knowledge and explicitly define the role of kernel theories in their meta-artefact design process.

6 Conclusion

In this paper, we presented an approach for using the grounded theory method to create kernel theories for design science processes. By introducing this approach, we explained and clarified the connection between descriptive and prescriptive knowledge. The processes that generate descriptive and prescriptive knowledge can sometimes be seen as mutually exclusive in research projects. Our main contribution is to clarify their relationships and demonstrate how both knowledge creation processes can be complementary to each other in design science research. Furthermore, we demonstrated the approach by using it to frame an ongoing research project in smart city service design.

Our contribution to the evolving body of knowledge of design science research is demonstrating how kernel theories generated with the grounded theory method can contribute to any artefact creation process, not only design theories. With this demonstrated approach we contribute to the Kuechler and Vaishnavi's theory generation framework [6], the line of research that discusses the use of descriptive knowledge in design science [3, 5, 7, 23, 28, 36, 37], and the line of research in meta-artefact design by Ostrowski and Helfert [8–11].

The approach presented in this paper can be considered a design science meta-artefact and we presented the first steps towards the its artificial validation. The approach requires further investigation and evaluation in order to establish its utility and thus the validity. If in the future a research project uses the approach with positive outcomes, that can be considered naturalistic evaluation and will eventually lead to the approach's full validation.

Acknowledgements. The work of the first author was supported by the Ulla Tuominen Foundation. This work was supported, in part, by Science Foundation Ireland grant 13/RC/2094 and co-funded under the European Regional Development Fund through the Southern & Eastern Regional Operational Programme to Lero - the Irish Software Research Centre (www.lero.ie).

References

1. Hevner, A.R., March, S.T., Park, J., Ram, S.: Design science in information systems research. MIS Q. **28**, 75–105 (2004)
2. Hevner, A.R.: The three cycle view of design science research. Scand. J. Inf. Syst. **19**, 87 (2007)
3. Gregor, S., Hevner, A.R.: Positioning and presenting design science research for maximum impact. MIS Q. **37**, 337–355 (2013)
4. Iivari, J.: A paradigmatic analysis of information systems as a design science. Scand. J. Inf. Syst. **19**, 5 (2007)
5. Gregor, S., Jones, D.: The anatomy of a design theory. J. Assoc. Inf. Syst. **8**, 312 (2007)
6. Kuechler, W., Vaishnavi, V.: A framework for theory development in design science research: multiple perspectives. J. Assoc. Inf. Syst. **13**, 395 (2012)
7. Kuechler, B., Vaishnavi, V.: On theory development in design science research: anatomy of a research project. Eur. J. Inf. Syst. **17**, 489–504 (2008)
8. Ostrowski, L., Helfert, M.: Business process modelling in design science paradigm. In: Helfert, M., Donnellan, B., Kenneally, J. (eds.) EDSS 2013. CCIS, vol. 447, pp. 111–122. Springer, Cham (2014). https://doi.org/10.1007/978-3-319-13936-4_10
9. Ostrowski, Ł., Helfert, M., Hossain, F.: A conceptual framework for design science research. In: Grabis, J., Kirikova, M. (eds.) BIR 2011. LNBIP, vol. 90, pp. 345–354. Springer, Heidelberg (2011). https://doi.org/10.1007/978-3-642-24511-4_27
10. Ostrowski, L., Helfert, M.: Reference model in design science research to gather and model information. In: AMCIS 2012 Proceedings (2012)
11. Ostrowski, L., Helfert, M., Xie, S.: A conceptual framework to construct an artefact for meta-abstract design knowledge in design science research. In: 2012 45th Hawaii International Conference on System Sciences, pp. 4074–4081 (2012)
12. Goldkuhl, G., Lind, M.: A multi-grounded design research process. In: Winter, R., Zhao, J. Leon, Aier, S. (eds.) DESRIST 2010. LNCS, vol. 6105, pp. 45–60. Springer, Heidelberg (2010). https://doi.org/10.1007/978-3-642-13335-0_4
13. Glaser, B., Strauss, A.L.: The Discovery of Grounded Theory: Strategies for Qualitative Research. Aldine, Chicago (1967)
14. Corbin, J.M., Strauss, A.: Grounded theory research: procedures, canons, and evaluative criteria. Qual. Sociol. **13**, 3–21 (1990)
15. Urquhart, C., Lehmann, H., Myers, M.D.: Putting the 'theory' back into grounded theory: guidelines for grounded theory studies in information systems. Inf. Syst. J. **20**, 357–381 (2010)
16. Pourzolfaghar, Z., Helfert, M.: Taxonomy of smart elements for designing effective services. In: AMCIS 2017 Proceedings (2017)
17. Knutas, A., Pourzolfaghar, Z., Helfert, M.: A meta-level design science process for integrating stakeholder needs. In: Proceedings of the International Conference on Computer-Human Interaction Research and Applications. Scitepress – Science and Technology Publications, Funchal (2017)

18. Hevner, A., Chatterjee, S.: Design Research in Information Systems. Springer, Boston (2010). https://doi.org/10.1007/978-1-4419-5653-8
19. Lee, A.S.: MIS quarterly's editorial policies and practices. MIS Q. **25**, iii–vii (2001)
20. Simon, H.A.: The Sciences of the Artificial. MIT Press, Cambridge (1996)
21. Cross, N.: Design/science/research: developing a discipline. In: Fifth Asian Design Conference: International Symposium on Design Science, Su Jeong Dang Printing Company, Seoul (2001)
22. Peffers, K., Tuunanen, T., Rothenberger, M.A., Chatterjee, S.: A design science research methodology for information systems research. J. Manag. Inf. Syst. **24**, 45–77 (2007)
23. Goldkuhl, G.: Design theories in information systems-a need for multi-grounding. JITTA: J. Inf. Technol. Theory Appl. **6**, 59 (2004)
24. Sun, Y., Kantor, P.B.: Cross-evaluation: a new model for information system evaluation. J. Am. Soc. Inf. Sci. Technol. **57**, 614–628 (2006)
25. Pries-Heje, J., Baskerville, R., Venable, J.: Strategies for design science research evaluation. In: ECIS 2008 Proceedings, pp. 1–12 (2008)
26. Venable, J.: A framework for design science research activities. In: Emerging Trends and Challenges in Information Technology Management: Proceedings of the 2006 Information Resource Management Association Conference, pp. 184–187. Idea Group Publishing (2006)
27. Martin, P.Y., Turner, B.A.: Grounded theory and organizational research. J. Appl. Behav. Sci. **22**, 141–157 (1986)
28. Adams, L.A., Courtney, J.F.: Achieving relevance in IS research via the DAGS framework. In: 2004 Proceedings of the 37th Annual Hawaii International Conference on System Sciences, pp. 10–pp. IEEE (2004)
29. Kinnunen, P., Simon, B.: Building theory about computing education phenomena: a discussion of grounded theory. In: Proceedings of the 10th Koli Calling International Conference on Computing Education Research, pp. 37–42. ACM, New York (2010)
30. Glaser, B.G.: Theoretical Sensitivity: Advances in the Methodology of Grounded Theory. Sociology Press, Mill Valley (1978)
31. Strauss, A.L.: Qualitative Analysis for Social Scientists. Cambridge University Press, Cambridge (1987)
32. Strauss, A., Corbin, J.M.: Basics of Qualitative Research: Grounded Theory Procedures and Techniques. Sage Publications Inc., Thousand Oaks (1990)
33. Gregor, S.: The nature of theory in information systems. MIS Q. **30**, 611–642 (2006)
34. Van de Ven, A.H.: Engaged Scholarship: A Guide for Organizational and Social Research. Oxford University Press, New York (2007)
35. Urquhart, C.: Grounded Theory for Qualitative Research: A Practical Guide. SAGE, Thousand Oaks (2012)
36. Gregory, R.W.: Design science research and the grounded theory method: Characteristics, differences, and complementary uses. In: Heinzl, A., Buxmann, P., Wendt, O., Weitzel, T. (eds.) Theory-Guided Modeling and Empiricism in Information Systems Research, pp. 111–127. Springer, Heidelberg (2011). https://doi.org/10.1007/978-3-7908-2781-1_6
37. Holmström, J., Ketokivi, M., Hameri, A.-P.: Bridging practice and theory: a design science approach. Decis. Sci. **40**, 65–87 (2009)
38. Merton, R.K.: Social Theory and Social Structure. Simon and Schuster, New York (1968)
39. Walls, J.G., Widmeyer, G.R., El Sawy, O.A.: Building an information system design theory for vigilant EIS. Inf. Syst. Res. **3**, 36–59 (1992)
40. Anthopoulos, L., Janssen, M., Weerakkody, V.: A unified smart city model (USCM) for smart city conceptualization and benchmarking. Int. J. Electron. Gov. Res. (IJEGR) **12**, 77–93 (2016)
41. Booch, G.: Enterprise architecture and technical architecture. IEEE Softw. **27**, 96 (2010)

42. Kondepudi, S.N., et al.: Smart sustainable cities analysis of definitions. The ITU-T Focus Group for Smart Sustainable Cities (2014)
43. Ferguson, D., Sairamesh, J., Feldman, S.: Open frameworks for information cities. Commun. ACM **47**, 45–49 (2004)
44. Weisman, R.: An Overview of TOGAF Version 9.1. Publ. by Open Gr. 43 (2011)

Usage Analytics: A Process to Extract and Analyse Usage Data to Understand User Behaviour in Cloud

Manoj Kesavulu[(⊠)] , Duc-Tien Dang-Nguyen[(⊠)] , Marija Bezbradica[(⊠)] ,
and Markus Helfert

Lero, School of Computing, Dublin City University, Dublin, Ireland
manoj.kesavulu2@mail.dcu.ie,
{duc-tien.dang-nguyen,marija.bezbradica,markus.helfert}@dcu.ie

Abstract. Usage in the software field deals with knowledge about how end-users use the application and how the application responds to the users' action. Understanding usage data can help developers optimise the application development process by prioritising the resources such as time, cost and man power on features of the application which are critical for the user. However, in a complex cloud computing environment, the process of extracting and analysing usage data is difficult since the usage data is spread across various front-end interfaces and back-end underlying infrastructural components of the cloud that host the application and are of different types and formats. In this paper, we propose usage analytics, a process to extract and analyse usage to understand the behavioural usage patterns of the user with the aim to identify features critical to user. We demonstrate how to identify the features in a cloud based application, how to extract and analyse the usage data to understand the user behaviour.

Keywords: Usage data · Data extraction · Analytics · Application · Features · Cloud · User behaviour and usage pattern

1 Introduction

Cloud computing is an emerging paradigm, bringing many advantages to both users and services providers while making dynamic platforms, cost-effective, flexible, on-demand resource provisioning, and many others. Consequently, there are significantly increasing developments for cloud computing infrastructures and platforms, from large high-tech enterprises such as Microsoft (with Microsoft Azure), Amazon (with Amazon EC2), and IBM (with IBM Cloud), to name a few. According to Forbes, by the end of 2018, spending on IT-as-a-Service for data centers, software and services will be $547B[1]. The number of Cloud-based services has increased rapidly and strongly, offering various advantages

---

[1] https://www.forbes.com/sites/louiscolumbus/2017/04/29/roundup-of-cloud-computing-forecasts-2017/#7155e14e31e8.

© Springer Nature Switzerland AG 2019
A. Holzinger et al. (Eds.): CHIRA 2017, CCIS 654, pp. 109–124, 2019.
https://doi.org/10.1007/978-3-030-32965-5_6

over traditional software including reducing time to benefit, scalability, accessing through various interfaces and so on. Unfortunately, difficulties in understanding the way different users using the applications and the provided resources for the cloud services still exist. Understanding usage data of an application has various uses such as to personalise the application according to the end-user's preferences [14], profiling users for security [1], improvement in marketing of software products [3] and to analyse the performance of the application in the deployed environment for maintenance purposes [2,12]. Normally, cloud providers and users use several monitoring and analytics tools to ensure the cloud services and the applications deployed on them execute as intended. Traditionally, the cloud provider (vendor) provides application performance management tools to monitor the status of the deployed applications. These tools provide mainly a vast amount of usage data of the resources used which can be turn into some knowledge for resource provisioning or error diagnostics in the cloud systems at the infrastructure and application level [8]. However, it is non-trivial to obtain user-related information, for example, user's behaviour, user's usage pattern, which features of the application are critical for a user, from the data extracted using existing APM tools. In order to analyse these information, advanced data analytics on extracted usage data is required [6].

In this study, we present a novel usage analytics process, explain and demonstrate how to extract and analyse usage in cloud services and applications that can help reveal behavioural indicators. Extraction of usage data of the features provided by the cloud applications could help software developers and architects to make an informed decision for the development/improvement of functionalities of the system according to end-user usage patterns. Typically, usage data consists of different types and formats of data extracted from multiple sources. Analytical solutions refer to the use of various analysis techniques and methods such as data mining, machine learning, reasoning, and other methods to extract useful knowledge and insights from large data set. For example, a company can use analysis techniques to understand customers' behaviour and predict how they are engaged or which customers are least likely to quit. These insights can be discovered via customers' profiles, memberships they subscribe to, or their generated content (comments, clicks, and other interactions). Developers can understand if some functions do not work properly via the usage data generated by the actions performed by the user with the application. User interests can be modelled by extracting browsing behaviour when accessing web application [7]. Such analytical solutions are considered as increasingly critical tools for modern enterprise to get an informational advantage, and have evolved from a matter of choice to a fundamental requirement in the present competitive business environments. Applying these solutions, thus, is a key to discover insights from the applications' usage. Every user has their own pattern when using an application or a service. Understanding these patterns could help to improve the service or discover the trends in advance. These patterns, can be discovered from the usage data.

In our previous work, the criteria for the usage data are defined and analyse the existing usage data extraction techniques according to the defined criteria and propose a usage data extraction framework [9]. We proposed **Usage Analytics**, a set of potential novel solutions that could help tackle various challenges in the cloud domain. We provided an overview of usage analytics in the cloud environment and proposed how to discover insights using these analytics solutions [6]. In this paper, we present the usage analytics process and provide the techniques for the key activities of the process and demonstrate using an experiment conducted.

Consequently, the aims of this paper are:

- To discuss the challenges in understanding the user behaviour in a cloud environment.
- To provide an overview of what is usage analytics in the cloud environment and demonstrate the key activities of the usage analytics process;
- To provide techniques that can be used to identify, extract and analyse the usage data.

The remainder of the paper is structured as follows: in section Sect. 2 we discuss the challenges in understanding user behaviour in cloud and discuss the concept of usage data with the focus on cloud applications. In Sect. 3, We present the Usage Analytics Process. In Sect. 4, we implement the usage analytics process explaining the key activities of the process with the aim to understand the user behaviour. In Sect. 5, we discuss the conclusions drawn and directions for the future work.

2   Related Work

User behaviour in the context of this research is defined as "the set of aggregated actions performed by user with the cloud application". Several studies exist on monitoring and analysing user behaviour for different purposes in the information systems domain. In [11], the authors provide a tool-kit that exploits the hardware sensors and software capabilities of contemporary mobile devices like PDAs and smartphones to capture objective data about human behaviour and social context together with objective data about application usage and highly subjective data about user experience. In [4], the authors show the importance of users' attitude towards the website and attitude towards the internet in explaining attitude towards the brand and consumer behaviour. Web mining techniques help in understanding the user access patterns in websites with the aim to recommend relevant topics and their placement on the website pages [13]. Understanding the changes in user behaviour can also help to make Application programming logic adaptive [5], the authors present and discuss a logic based approach for automatically learning and updating models for users from their observed behaviour. It is worth noting that these usage data potentially can be exploited in situation-emotional analytics [10], which aims at recognizing the emotions and changes of software situations in order to improve the quality and user experience levels. These emotional information are now extracted via external biometric recording devices, e.g., recording devices that record the eye and gaze-tracking signal. We firmly believe that, usage information at the application levels, will be very useful for this type of learning and potentially can replace eye and gaze-tracking information.

User behaviour can be understood by analysing usage data and can various data sources in cloud, and the major challenge is they can be in any form and format, which brings many challenges for analysis. The main questions for usage data extraction is what usage data should be extracted and how to map the raw usage data with the right applications or services. Considering the multi-tenant architecture of the cloud, different applications share the same physical and virtual resources. This raises challenge as in how to separate and extract the logs that represent each application from the instance (VM) co-hosting the applications. Another important challenge is handling with different contextual information. A system usually has a lot of branches, and thus the systems behaviors may be quite different under different input data or environmental conditions. Knowing the execution behaviour under different inputs or configurations can greatly help system operators to understand system behaviors. However, there may be a large number of different combinations of inputs or parameters under different system behaviors. Such complexity poses difficulties for analyzing contextual information related to the state of interest. In order to understand user behavior, descriptive statistics, e.g., mean, total, standard variation, most frequent value, etc., are typically used to obtain meaningful insights such as the basic behaviors of the users. These information can be also used to classify the user based on the correlation and demographic similarities among them. In order to understand the patterns from user behavior, we propose to exploit all of the usage data from multiple layers of the cloud environment, usage data of a cloud-based application is spread across front-end interfaces (web-browser, smart phone app/client and command-line interface) and the back-end (server instance and database instance) in a cloud environment [9] and formulate as the transition states of a graph. This type of graph can be used to mine execution patterns and to model relationships among different user behavior patterns. This kind of approach can also be used to discover some problems under some specific context. To discover these contextual factors, we propose to use the decision trees to learn the conditions, which allows us to determine any possible connections between the contexts and change in behavior of the user. In this study, we focus to exploit the data in application logs and refer to the work in [6] as shown in Fig. 1, where the authors have classified the usage data sources at the back-end of cloud into three groups, coming from three main sources, as follows: the system logs from the cloud services from the back-end of the cloud system, the application logs, and the logs from the virtual machines (VMs). As discussed earlier, the usage data could be extracted from various sources in a cloud environment and these data are of different type and formats. Hence, usage data has to be classified according to categories. Table 1 provides a information on how usage data could be classified (refer [9] for a deeper discussion of classification).

Table 1. Usage data classification (Source [9]).

Who is using the application	(a) User ID
	(b) IP address
Where the application is being hosted	(a) Web server
	(b) Database
What the end user does	(a) Application
	(b) Page
	(c) Method
	(d) Function
	(e) Button that is accessed
	(f) Action that is performed
When the user performs the operation	(a) Date and time
	(b) Session ID
How long it takes to complete the operation	(a) Duration
	(b) Query duration
Operation details	(a) Errors
	(b) Background tasks
	(c) Number of records loaded
What application features are used by the user and how	(a) Clickstream
	(b) View
	(c) Focus
	(d) API calls

Usage data in a cloud environment can be mainly divided into three categories: 1. System logs contain a wealth of information to help manage systems. Most systems print out logs during their executions to record system runtime actions and states that can directly reflect system runtime behaviours. System developers and architects usually use these logs to track a system to detect and diagnose system anomalies.

2. The second type of this data is the user-level usage data generated as a result of user interaction with a cloud-based application. Some examples of usage data are application logs, for example the assessment data (wiki, forum, message), the activity data (clicks, time spent), server logs, and so on. They can be extracted by the applications themselves or via Web cookies (from web browser). Such data in the cloud is spread across various interfaces such as Web browser, mobile applications and command line interfaces on the front-end and server and database on the back-end.

3. The last type of usage data is the VM logs, typically generated from the VMs running the applications or services. This type of logs contains the usage of the CPU, memories, as well as running tasks, time of starting and stopping

and others. Figure 1 shows a summary of the three main sources of usage data in the back-end of a cloud environment.

In this paper, we consider application logs at the back-end as the usage data source. The application logs reveal information such as:

– IP address of the user
– HTTP request and responses between the browser and the application server running in the VM
– Timestamp
– Application events triggered by user
– Errors and warnings
– Application resource access
– Diagnostics data
– Network configurations
– Database requests and responses.

In the next section, we present the usage analytics process and explain how the usage data are identified, tools and techniques used for extraction, how the extracted usage data could be analysed to identify the behavioural usage patterns and discuss how to evaluate the usage data and the usage analytics process.

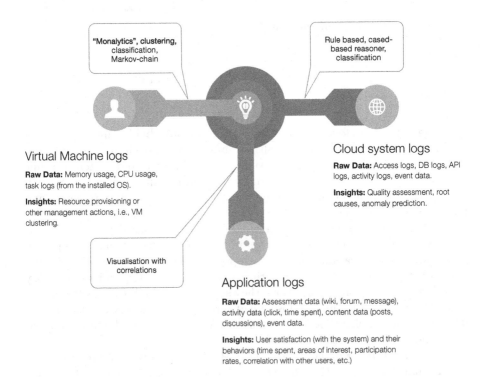

Fig. 1. Three main sources of usage data in cloud-based environment (Source: [6]).

3   Usage Analytics Process

Usage analytics process consists of steps explaining how to identify, extract and analyse the usage data with the aim to understand how users of an application use the features provided by the application. A high-level diagram of the usage analytics process is represented in Fig. 2.

Fig. 2. Experimental setup for Usage Analytics.

The first step is to classify the usage data which helps to know who is the user, what the user does, when does the user perform an action and so on. Refer to Table 1 in Sect. 2 for the usage data classification. The second step is to identify the features provided by the application. In order to identify the feature, it is essential to investigate the application architecture, identify the functionalities of the application, actions a users can perform, investigate the application catalogue provided by the developers and test the application for any features missing in the catalogue and then finally build a list of the features identified. The third step is to identify the usage data sources, it includes exploring the available usage data sources as shown in Fig. 1 in Sect. 2 while comparing the usage data classification as discussed in the first step. The fourth step includes carefully exploring the usage data source and identifying the format and type of the usage data to identify the user, action performed, time when the action performed and so on. The final step is to analyse the data, it includes using statistical analysis techniques to understand which feature was most used by which user, if the user consistent with accessing a particular feature, what is the frequency of the access of a feature and so on. This helps identifying distinguishing feature usage patterns of a user. Based on the different feature usage patterns exhibited by an user, we can identify which features are critical for the user.

4   Implementation

In this section, we present the experimental setup for the usage analytics process with the open-source application "Odoo Notes app"[2] chosen as the use-case. Odoo is a set of open-source range of easy to use business applications that form a complete suite of tools to accompany any business need. It is used by over 3.7 million users and around 950 business partners. Odoo notes is an online collaboration task management and to-do application. Users of this application are provided with a kanban-style dashboard to create, organise and edit notes. A complete set of functionalities provided this application is discussed in Sect. 4.2. The focus of this research is to extract and analyse usage data generated when user interact with the application through a browser.

---

[2] https://apps.odoo.com/apps/online/note/.

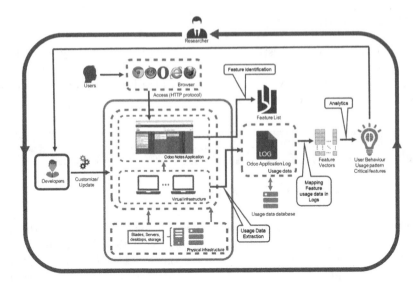

Fig. 3. Experimental setup for Usage Analytics.

4.1 Experimental Setup

The Odoo Notes application (community edition version 10) is deployed as a service in a virtual machine running Ubuntu 16.10 LTS operating system to simulate the nature of the cloud environment. Users access the application through as browser over the internet. Application logs are generated and stored in the VM hosting the application. Odoo Notes logs contain information such as Timestamp, HTTP requests and responses, Database requests and responses, IP address, Event name, Object ID and so on. Figure 3 shows the overall picture of Usage Analytics process. The first step in the process is to identify the list of features provided by the application.

4.2 Application Features Identification

Odoo notes is an online collaborative task management and to-do application. Users can create, edit and organise "notes" (similar to a sticky-note) in a kanban style dashboard. Users also have an option to share the notes with other users and invite other users to work together in a collaborative manner. Users can add comments to the notes, send private and broadcast messages to other users. A complete list of features provided by Notes application is available in the Odoo website. For the purpose of this study, we have carefully tested each feature and chosen only those features that a user explicitly can interact. This filtered set of features is shown in Table 2. The features F1–F17 are defined by the developer, features f18–F21 are manually identified by testing the application execution. We are aware of the possibility that the application may contain more features and many other features may be developed and implemented in the newer versions. But, in this paper, for the demonstration purpose, only the features listed in Table 2 are considered.

The focus of this research is to understand the user behaviour by analysing user interactions with the application. Feature F17 refers to a notification to the user about other users who are active. Since users do not have an option to interact with this feature of the application, it is neglected in this study. An interesting point to note is that the features listed here are initially defined by the developers of the application. However, we are aware of the fact that there could be other features being identified and categorised in the later versions of the application. Usage Analytics process is designed in a way to accommodate additional features being added to the list. Once the list of features to focus on is prepared, the next step is to extract the usage data.

Table 2. List of features of Odoo Notes Application.

#	Feature	Description
F1	Create stages (Columns)	Break down your to-do list into stages which will be converted to columns into your dashboard
F2	Create notes	Add notes to your stages. Each note correspond to a mini-project that you will move from one stage to another as your project moves forward
F3	Kanban view	Drag and drop notes easily from one stage to another in the kanban view
F4	Text layout	Insert text styles like headers bold, italic, lists and fonts with a simple WYSIWYG editor
F5	File attachments	Attach text files image files document files to your notes
F6	Tags	Add tags to your notes for a clear organization
F7	Filters and groups	Search notes easily with smart filters
F8	Colors	Group your notes by color as a way to categorize your tasks. There are 9 colors to choose from and a colorless option
F9	Import	Upload any text file or document to your notes
F10	Export	Export notes as HTML plain text or DocuWiki text documents
F11	Invite people	Add coworkers to your notes so they can follow the discussions and receive notifications
F12	Authorship color	Every author typing some text in a note has a different background color to show who wrote what. You can link a name to a color

Table 2. (*continued*)

#	Feature	Description
F13	Timeline slider	See the history of changes made to a note through a timeline from first to last sentence
F14	Share	Easily share your notes with your colleagues by sending them as link or embed URL
F15	Access Settings	Choose what others can do with your notes by granting viewing or editing access
F16	Chat	Enable chat for real time discussion with the people following your notes
F17	Show Connected Users*	See who is connected to your notes right now
F18	Delete a Note	Deletes a note, including the comments, attachments and tags attached
F19	Edit Note	Open the note in edit mode. Change the title, text and add comments
F20	Duplicate Note	Create a duplicate copy of the note in the same stage (column)
F21	Post Comment	Add comment to a note, all collaborators can view the comments

4.3 Usage Data Extraction

The Usage data extraction step includes identification of the usage data sources, identification of the usage data and the corresponding data extraction process. In a cloud environment, some of the typical usage data sources are application logs, application cache, server logs, cloud system logs, Application Programming Interface (API) event data, network logs on the back-end and browser cache, browser cookies, desktop client log, mobile app logs, mobile system logs and so on. Depending on the type of usage data and the purpose of analysis, appropriate usage data source can be considered. In this paper, we focus on application logs as the usage data source, type 2, as discussed in Sect. 2. Odoo notes application log entries contain the following information, explained using a small subset of the log data as shown in Log 1.1:

Log 1.1. Odoo Notes sample application log entries.

```
2018-03-28 12:24:10,966 8970 INFO ? werkzeug:
    ↪ 136.206.48.84 - - [28/Mar/2018 12:24:10] "GET /
    ↪ web_editor/static/src/js/transcoder.js HTTP/1.1"
    ↪ 200 -
2018-03-28 12:24:11,256 8970 DEBUG Odoo_Database odoo.
    ↪ api: call ir.ui.view().read_template(u'web_editor
    ↪ .colorpicker')
2018-03-28 12:24:11,260 8970 INFO Odoo_Database
    ↪ werkzeug: 136.206.48.84 - - [28/Mar/2018
    ↪ 12:24:11] "POST /web/dataset/call HTTP/1.1" 200 -
2018-03-28 12:24:11,309 8970 INFO Odoo_Database
    ↪ werkzeug: 136.206.48.84 - - [28/Mar/2018
    ↪ 12:24:11] "POST /web/webclient/translations HTTP
    ↪ /1.1" 200 -
2018-03-28 12:24:11,324 8970 INFO ? werkzeug:
    ↪ 136.206.48.84 - - [28/Mar/2018 12:24:11] "GET /
    ↪ web_editor/static/src/xml/editor.xml?debug
    ↪ =1522239851310 HTTP/1.1" 200 -
2018-03-28 12:33:46,695 8970 DEBUG Odoo_Database odoo.
    ↪ api: call note.tag(4,).read([u'name', u'color'])
```

The first and second fields in all the log entries represent the time stamp. The keywords *INFO, DEBUG* represent the level of logging, other possible options are *CRITICAL, ERROR and WARN*. The fourth field represents the target data store, a "?" symbol represents requests to load web-pages and web scripts. The name of the database in this sample is "Odoo_Database". The keyword "werkzeug" is the name of the logger tool. The next field shows the IP address of the user (or the person who made the request, for example, administrator of the application). Next field of importance is the HTTP request and response between the browser and the application server along with the response code. One interesting fact to notice here is that Odoo application logs can configured to capture the API calls which reveal a vast amount of information about features such as object ID of the elements (for example, ID of the tag is 4), operation performed (for example, the last line of the log entry represents read operation with the variables - the user defined name of the tag and the colour assigned by user to the note).

User actions can be identified by analysing the logs which helps reveal individual user's pattern of interactions with the application. In the next section we discuss how the logs are analysed to reveal usage patterns of the users.

4.4 Analysis

The first step in analysing the usage data is to map the feature data to the log entries. This step involves identifying the keywords in the log entries that refer to the actions performed by the user to the keywords in the log entries. A mapping file is created to aid this purpose as shown in 1.2.

Log 1.2. Feature mapping.

```
F3: Reorder / rearrange note
2018-03-27 12:58:22,875 20602 INFO Odoo_Database
    ↪ werkzeug: 136.206.48.84 - - [27/Mar/2018
    ↪ 12:58:22] "POST /web/dataset/resequence HTTP/1.1"
    ↪ 200 -

F18: Delete a note
2018-03-27 13:48:15,166 20602 INFO Odoo_Database odoo.
    ↪ models.unlink: User #1 deleted note.note records
    ↪ with IDs: [33]

F19: Create a new note
2018-03-27 13:49:23,804 20602 INFO Odoo_Database
    ↪ werkzeug: 136.206.48.84 - - [27/Mar/2018
    ↪ 13:49:23] "POST /web/dataset/call_kw/note.note/
    ↪ create HTTP/1.1" 200 -

F20: Duplicate a note
2018-03-27 13:51:30,902 20602 INFO Odoo_Database
    ↪ werkzeug: 136.206.48.84 - - [27/Mar/2018
    ↪ 13:51:30] "POST /web/dataset/call_kw/note.note/
    ↪ copy HTTP/1.1" 200 -

F18: Edit note
2018-03-27 13:52:44,783 20602 INFO Odoo_Database
    ↪ werkzeug: 136.206.48.84 - - [27/Mar/2018
    ↪ 13:52:44] "POST /web/dataset/call_kw/note.note/
    ↪ read HTTP/1.1" 200 -
2018-03-27 13:52:44,806 20602 INFO Odoo_Database
    ↪ werkzeug: 136.206.48.84 - - [27/Mar/2018
    ↪ 13:52:44] "POST /mail/read_followers HTTP/1.1"
    ↪ 200 -
2018-03-27 13:52:44,831 20602 INFO Odoo_Database
    ↪ werkzeug: 136.206.48.84 - - [27/Mar/2018
    ↪ 13:52:44] "POST /web/dataset/search_read HTTP
    ↪ /1.1" 200 -
```

```
2018-03-27 13:52:55,493 20602 INFO Odoo_Database
   ↪ werkzeug: 136.206.48.84 - - [27/Mar/2018
   ↪ 13:52:55] "POST /web/dataset/call_kw/note.note/
   ↪ write HTTP/1.1" 200 -

F21: Open commenting in note - loads users list
2018-03-27 13:54:57,434 20602 INFO Odoo_Database
   ↪ werkzeug: 136.206.48.84 - - [27/Mar/2018
   ↪ 13:54:57] "POST /web/dataset/call_kw/note.note/
   ↪ message_get_suggested_recipients HTTP/1.1" 200 -

F21: Post comment in note
2018-03-27 13:56:18,848 20602 INFO Odoo_Database
   ↪ werkzeug: 136.206.48.84 - - [27/Mar/2018
   ↪ 13:56:18] "POST /web/dataset/call_kw/note.note/
   ↪ message_post HTTP/1.1" 200 -

F6: Create new tag in note
2018-03-27 13:59:29,608 20602 INFO Odoo_Database
   ↪ werkzeug: 136.206.48.84 - - [27/Mar/2018
   ↪ 13:59:29] "POST /web/dataset/call_kw/note.tag/
   ↪ name_create HTTP/1.1" 200 -
2018-03-27 13:59:32,082 20602 INFO Odoo_Database
   ↪ werkzeug: 136.206.48.84 - - [27/Mar/2018
   ↪ 13:59:32] "POST /web/dataset/call_kw/note.tag/
   ↪ create HTTP/1.1" 200 -

F6: Add new tag
2018-03-27 14:10:14,925 20602 INFO Odoo_Database
   ↪ werkzeug: 136.206.48.84 - - [27/Mar/2018
   ↪ 14:10:14] "POST /web/dataset/call_kw/note.tag/
   ↪ read HTTP/1.1" 200 -
2018-03-27 14:10:14,929 20602 INFO Odoo_Database
   ↪ werkzeug: 136.206.48.84 - - [27/Mar/2018
   ↪ 14:10:14] "POST /web/menu/load_needaction HTTP
   ↪ /1.1" 200 -
```

The mapping file will help identify the keywords to search in the logs file for entries that reveal the actions performed by users. Google's colab tool[3] is used for identifying the moments at which a specific user performed a specific task. Colab tool is built on Jupyter notebook[4], which is an open-source web application used for data cleaning and transformation, numerical simulation, statistical modelling, data visualization, machine learning, and so on. Keywords identified

---

[3] https://colab.research.google.com.

[4] http://jupyter.org.

from the mapping file are used to search the log. The keywords in the odoo notes application logs are generally found in in the HTTP POST request and API call fields. *Feature F3: Reorder/rearrange note* is represented in the log entry by the keyword "resequence". *Feature F18: Delete a note* can be identified using the keyword "delete note.note" and the log entry also provides the ID of the note deleted. In this sample log, the ID of the note deleted is "33". Similarly, *Feature F19: Create a note* can be identified by the keyword "note.note/create". While these are keywords are simple to recognise by their names, some keywords are difficult to identify. For example, the log entry for the *Feature F21: Open comment box in note* do not use keywords such as comment or open in the HTTP request. However, the keywords "note.note/message_get_suggested_recipients" reveal that a comment box was opened by the user as the application loaded the message recipient suggestions. Hence, a mapping file should be carefully created by anticipating the actions performed and understanding the programming logic of the application.

Statistical analysis could be used to identify the frequency by which a user accessed a feature, amount of time spent using a feature, consistency in accessing the feature and so on. Each feature can be ranked for each user or a group of users' usage pattern, which is yet to be implemented and tested, one of the aims of our future work. Snapshots of the user browser window are captured with the frequency of four snapshots per minute. The behavioural patterns of a users resulted from the analysis could be validated using the snapshots captured. Machine learning techniques can be used to cluster users who exhibit similar behavioural patterns, correlation between user clusters can be understood to help improve the ranking of the features. Developers can use this knowledge about the criticality of the features from the user's perspective to optimise the development of the application.

5   Conclusion and Future Work

We presented the usage analytics process, discussed and demonstrated the key activities: Feature Identification, Usage Data Extraction, Analysis and discussed how the usage data and the process of usage data extraction and analysis can be evaluated. The usage analytics process demonstrated with an experiment in this paper shows how to successfully understand behavioural usage patterns of the user in a cloud environment. The behavioural indicators could help the developers of the applications in cloud to optimise the software development process by prioritising the development resources to the features critical to the user.

For our future work, we aim to (1) test this experiment with users and implement the evaluation plan discussed in Sect. 5; (2) use machine learning algorithms to identify more behavioural indicators by analysing the correlation between the group of user exhibiting similar usage patterns; (3) include usage data from other relevant usage data sources (for example, browser sessions, cookies etc.) to improve the proposed extraction and analysis process.

Acknowledgements. This work was supported with the financial support of the Science Foundation Ireland grant 13/RC/2094 and co-funded under the European Regional Development Fund through the Southern & Eastern Regional Operational Programme to Lero - the Irish Software Research Centre (www.lero.ie).

References

1. Al-Bayati, B., Clarke, N., Dowland, P.: Adaptive behavioral profiling for identity verification in cloud computing: a model and preliminary analysis. GSTF J. Comput. (JoC) **5**(1), 21 (2016)
2. Bezemer, C.P., Zaidman, A., Platzbeecker, B., Hurkmans, T., Hart, A.: Enabling multi-tenancy: an industrial experience report. In: IEEE International Conference on Software Maintenance, pp. 1–8, September 2010. https://doi.org/10.1109/ICSM.2010.5609735
3. Bucklin, R.E., Sismeiro, C.: Click here for internet insight: advances in clickstream data analysis in marketing. J. Interact. Mark. **23**(1), 35–48 (2009)
4. Castañeda, J.A., Rodríguez, M.A., Luque, T.: Attitudes' hierarchy of effects in online user behaviour. Online Inf. Rev. **33**(1), 7–21 (2009). https://doi.org/10.1108/14684520910944364. http://www.emeraldinsight.com/doi/10.1108/14684520910944364
5. Corapi, D., Ray, O., Russo, A., Bandara, A.K., Lupu, E.C.: Learning rules from user behaviour. In: Iliadis, Tsoumakasis, Vlahavas, Bramer (eds.) Artificial Intelligence Applications and Innovations III, vol. 296, pp. 459–468. Springer, Boston (2009). https://doi.org/10.1007/978-1-4419-0221-4_54
6. Dang-Nguyen, D.T., Kesavulu, M., Helfert, M.: Usage analytics: research directions to discover insights from cloud-based applications. In: International Conference on Smart Cities and Green ICT Systems (SMARTGREENS) (2018, accepted)
7. Gasparetti, F.: Modeling user interests from web browsing activities. Data Min. Knowl. Disc. **31**(2), 1–46 (2016). https://doi.org/10.1007/s10618-016-0482-x
8. Kesavulu, M., Dang-Nguyen, D.T., Helfert, M., Bezbradica, M.: An overview of user-level usage monitoring in cloud environment. In: The UK Academy for Information Systems (UKAIS) (2018)
9. Kesavulu, M., Helfert, M., Bezbradica, M.: A usage-based data extraction framework for cloud-based application - an human-computer interaction approach. In: International Conference on Computer-Human Interaction Research and Applications (CHIRA), Madeira, Portugal (2017)
10. Märtin, C., Herdin, C., Engel, J.: Model-based user-interface adaptation by exploiting situations, emotions and software patterns. In: International Conference on Computer-Human Interaction Research and Applications (2017)
11. Mulder, I., Ter Hofte, G.H., Kort, J.: SocioXensor: Measuring user behaviour and user eXperience in conteXt with mobile devices. In: Proceedings of Measuring Behavior, pp. 355–358, January 2005
12. Petruch, K., Tamm, G., Stantchev, V.: Deriving in-depth knowledge from IT-performance data simulations. Int. J. Knowl. Soc. Res. **3**(2), 13–29 (2012). https://doi.org/10.4018/jksr.2012040102. http://services.igi-global.com/resolvedoi/resolve.aspx?doi=10.4018/jksr.2012040102

13. Xu, G., Zhang, Y., Yi, X.: Modelling user behaviour for Web recommendation using LDA model. In: Proceedings - 2008 IEEE/WIC/ACM International Conference on Web Intelligence and Intelligent Agent Technology - Workshops, WI-IAT Workshops 2008, pp. 529–532 (2008). https://doi.org/10.1109/WIIAT.2008.313
14. Yang, J., et al.: Multimedia recommendation and transmission system based on cloud platform. Future Gener. Comput. Syst. **70**, 94–103 (2017)

On the Efficient Graph Representation of Collinear Relation in the 3D Shape Grammars

Kamila Kotulska[✉]

AGH University of Science and Technology, Mickiewicza 30, 30-059 Krakow, Poland
kotulska@agh.edu.pl

Abstract. Shape grammars are a powerful, generative approach to description, interpretation and evaluation of many designs. There are many examples of their successfully application for architectural 3D systems. Our research has been inspired by Antonio Gaudi's Sagrada Familia designs. The complication of such a project developed in thousands overlapping planes, needs process automation with the help of formal method and artificial intelligence. However the successful examples are restricted to small graphs or those with reduced numbers of rules and shapes Practical large implementation of such a system fails with respect of problems related to computational and spatial efficiency. In the second case the crucial is the correct representation of basic terms such as efficient graph representation of the collinear segments. Such a representation is proposed and compared with two most popular ones basing on a classical application of shape grammars pattern – Stiny's Chinese lattice design. The problems of its application in 3D is also considered.

Keywords: Shape grammars · Graph representation · Computational model(s) · Computer-aided conceptual design

1 Introduction

Building Sagrada Familia is one of the biggest and greatest challenge for architects, designers and constructors these days. The design is not only extremely complicated, but it is also unfinished. The great Antonio Gaudi has passed away before he had shown to the world the complete idea of art of his life. The only way to find out how he would have finished the Sagrada Famillia is using Artificial Intelligence to create his vision.

Shape Grammars have been introduced in 1971 by Stiny [21] and further developed by himself. Stiny defined them as a "set of rules of transformation applied recursively to an initial form, generating new forms" [19]. Since then, they have been used as a powerful generative approach to description, interpretation and evaluation of many designs. For over 45 years, the notation of the formalism has been significantly changed and developed. Despite that, shape

A. Holzinger et al. (Eds.): CHIRA 2017, CCIS 654, pp. 125–138, 2019.
https://doi.org/10.1007/978-3-030-32965-5_7

grammars were used constantly as a rule-based system for describing and generating designs [11,17].

Over years Shape Grammars has become a great, powerful tool to generate and describe projects from many various arenas. In 2015 Knight and Stiny [9], created classification distinguishes seven areas of application of shape grammars:

- Painting [10]
- Product design. [7]
- Area of craft [16]
- Mechanical design [1]
- Landscape design [20]
- Area of architecture [3]
- Urban design [2]

Common assumption for all of these areas is a participation of human during design process.

During our work on the project inspired by Antonio Gaudi's the greatest projects we have realized that billions of elements creates Sagrada Familia. Such a big amount of elements has brought us to conclusion that human needs to be replaced by Artificial Intelligence. Although, during the work on billions of elements AI would have better processing efficiency, in addition to human will have low level of intuition, esthetic or abstract thinking. Those three elements are important part of the job for any designers. That is why Shape Grammars supported by Artificial Intelligence needs to be based on a formal definitions used by the system.

Analysis of the mentioned examples leads us to the conclusion that Shape Grammars can be successfully applied in many fields. However, the graph structures, which formally represent problems, are based on small graphs or have limited numbers of rules.

During our work on the project inspired by Antonio Gaudi's designs we have noticed a serious problem with graph processing efficiency. We work on different types of structures, which are described by large numbers of nodes. The project requires representation of thousands or even millions of edges, nodes and shapes which are not represented by lines. Even the most advanced among the exiting methods are incapable to process such vast collections data. Real-life application of shape grammars demands their efficient implementation for shapes consisting of thousands of elements.

Translation of shapes into graph grammars requires many problems to be solved, including:

- Complexity reduction of designation of the left-hand side of transformation rules: In a general case, it is an NP-complete problem, just like subgraph isomorphism. But with some restrictions on the application rule form and the generated graph structure, it can be solved in a polynomial time (cf. [4]).
- Introduction of a mechanism of parallel application of the transformation rules with implicit synchronization; cf. [13].

However, the most basic and yet still open problem is proper and efficient representation of the shape elements. Lets note that introduction of third dimension strengthens the importance of effective representation of the collinear points.

The scope of the paper is as follows: the application of shape grammars in 3D design is considered in Sect. 2, comparison of collinear segments implementation is presented in Sect. 3 and practical aspect of application of the VG-x collinearity representation [12] are presented in Sect. 4.

2 3D Shape Generation

Shape grammars are used to generation of the design very complex objects. Muller and Wonka [15] presented a building generated with snap lined which were used during the construction. A simple building is made up of many basic shapes, which are determined by numerous planes.

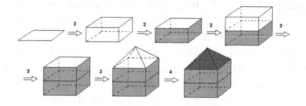

Fig. 1. Sequence of Shape Grammars transformations.

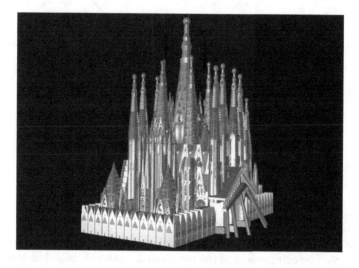

Fig. 2. Sagrada Familia generated based on Shape Grammars.

Since a few years our department has developed The Virtual Gaudi Project. The general idea is to formally describe the existing works of Antonio Gaudi, analyses them using various AI systems and finally start to generate a new design in the "Gaudi style". Antonio Gaudi's style is known because consist of millions of details and combing multiple planes. For example his greatest design Sagrada Famila has hundreds of thousand planes, and collinear points.

The Shape Grammars, the genarated 3D shapes are represented as a composition of the basic shapes like hexahedron, tetrahedron, cone, etc. These basic shapes were formed as a result of intersection of planes. Such a composition is presented in Fig. 1.

Consequently such a transfomations generate the designs of the complex object [14], that are shown in Fig. 2 shows that even such a complex design as Sagrada Familia can be generated with basic elements like hexahedron, tetrahedron etc. Although, in such a complex project it is extremely important to find optimal graph representation. Number of planes and collinear points have led us to conclusion that efficient graph representation is a principal requirement for The Virtual Gaudi Project. The basic assumption is that optimal representation in 3D is naturally based on optimal 2D representation. But is more complicated

The shape graph presented in Fig. 3 consists of two overlapping squares (basic elements). In this example, the line segment (a, b) has been split into three collinear segments (the other line segments also have been split). The representation of relations among them and segment (a, b) has a strong influence on the implementation of the shape grammar. In a 3D case the intersection of the cube through plane Π designate 4 new segments.

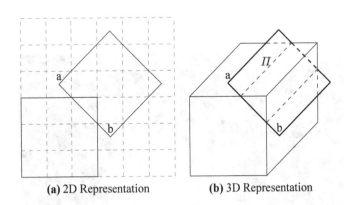

(a) 2D Representation   (b) 3D Representation

Fig. 3. Collinearity problem in Shape Grammars.

This problem has been considered by Kotulska [12] that propose new representation that was inspired by the presented by Grasl and Economou [5] and Keles et al. [8]. The comparison of the mentioned method is based on the classical Stiny shape grammar application for Chinese ice-ray lattice design [18].

3   Comparison of Collinear Segments Implementation

One of the most important problems associated with graph representation of shapes is the representation of collinear shapes in a way that allows to use them for the analogical relations as Beziér curve elements. The maximum line segments are a set of lines created by combining all collinear line segments which touch or overlap. The most straightforward approach is to map points to the nodes and segments to the edges. In such a representation, if a line is divided into several segments by a crossing line, it is difficult to designate the other collinear segments. Note that, two or more connected collinear segments can appear in the transformation rule as one segment. To overcome this problem, three representation are considered and compared.

Keles et al. [8] join all node pairs in such lines. Unfortunately, this approach results in creation of too many edges. For n points along the line, $n \cdot (n-1)/2$ edges have to be created. Thus, even for a small grid of lines (over a dozen intersecting lines), like the one in Stiny's ice-ray [18], a large number of edges is generated: 1653 edges for Chengtu Szeehwan, 1825 AD and 1392 edges for Hanchow, Szechwan 1875 AD.

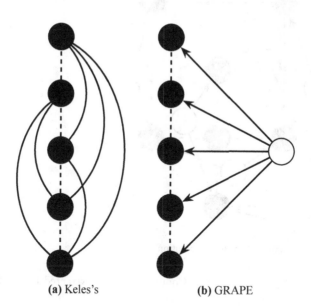

(a) Keles's   **(b)** GRAPE

Fig. 4. GRAPE long line representation (extracted from [12]).

Grasl and Economou analyse 7 other representations and finally introduce the representation in which both points and segment lines are represented as nodes (points as a black nodes and lines as a white nodes). The collinear 5-segment line in both approaches is presented in Fig. 4b and a.

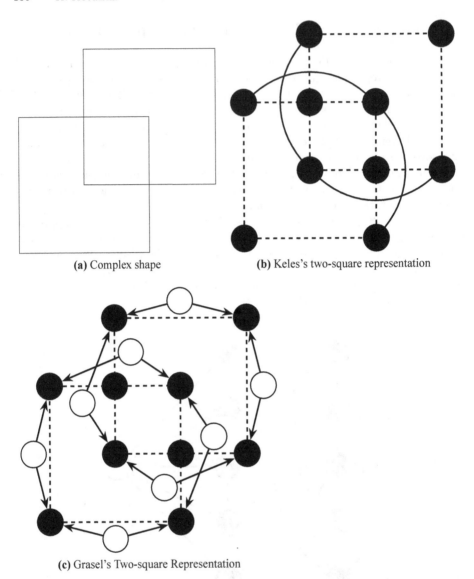

(a) Complex shape   (b) Keles's two-square representation

(c) Grasel's Two-square Representation

Fig. 5. Representation of a Complex Shapes (extracted from [12]).

The efficiency of the collinear representations should be verified on more complex situations as the one presented in Fig. 5a. This representation is efficient for collinear lines, but we have to analyse it in the entire context of the generated shapes.

As already mentioned, two opposite graph representations of the collinearity problem have been considered in literature. The first one has been proposed by Keles [8]. He mentioned that shape nodes are represented as graph nodes and shapes are represented as edges (A attributes are also remembered in edges). The representation of collinear segments defined using 5 nodes is illustrated in Fig. 4a. We will have 10 collinear segments and the same number of edges. A more compact representation suggested by Grasl and Economu [5] introduces white nodes for representation of the shape edges. The representation of collinear segments defined by 5 nodes is illustrated in Fig. 4b. The A attributes will be remembered in white nodes. Two segments are collinear if their end nodes are connected with the same white node.

The advantage of the Grasl representation is not obvious in the case of more complex shapes, such as the one presented in Fig. 5a.

Keles's representation of the shapes presented in Fig. 5a is presented in Fig. 5b.

Grasl's representation of the same shape presented in Fig. 5c is not that simple. The shape is now represented using 18 nodes and 28 edges, while in Keles's approach, the same shape is represented using 10 nodes and 16 edges.

Lack of clear advantage one of the mentioned representations causes the necessity of looking for of another solution. Kotulska [12] suggests the merging of the both presented representations. In a VG-2 representation (as abbreviation of Virtual Gaudi notation) for two collinear segments, we will use direct inline edges (as in Keles's solution) and if there are more segments, Grasl's representation will be used. In VG-3 representation two or tree collinear segments, we will use direct inline edges (as in Keles's solution) and if there are more segments, Grasl's representation will be used.

3.1 Comparison Based on Chinese Lattice

It is obvious that composed artworks consist of millions of details. Because of that, efficient graph representation is a principal requirement for this idea. In contrast to human perception, which prefers one consistent representation of the problem, the graph grammar formal notation has no problem in describing the same concept in two or more ways, Fig. 2 depending on some parameters e.g. the size of the represented elements. This fact is the basis for the proposed solution.

Stine [18] analyses several examples of Chinese lattice design to show the expressiveness and capabilities of shape grammars. In this paper we will consider the Chengtu Szeehwan, from 1800 AD (see Fig. 6a) and from 1825 AD (see Fig. 6b), as well as Hanchow, Szechwan from 1875 AD (see Fig. 6c).

Table 1 shows number of lines consisting from n collinear nodes in the designs from 1800, 1825 and 1875 years.

Lets start the analyse these four approaches on the Chinese lattice designs.

In Chengtu, Szechwan 1800 AD design we have 167 (black) nodes and 262 direct (dashed) edges. The (white) nodes, additional edges and the overall number of the given method of representation are presented in Table 2a.

In Chengtu, Szechwan 1825 AD design we have 237 (black) nodes and 262 direct (dashed) edges. The (white) nodes, additional edges and the overall number of the given method of representation are presented in Table 2b. In Hanchow, Szechwan 1875 AD design we have 165 (black) nodes and 276 direct (dashed) edges.

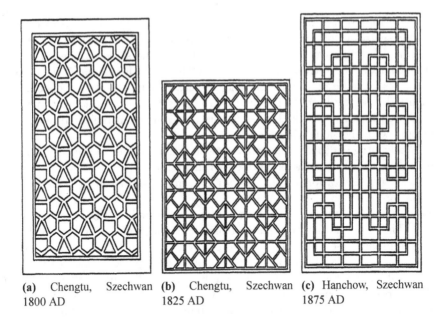

(a) Chengtu, Szechwan (b) Chengtu, Szechwan (c) Hanchow, Szechwan
1800 AD   1825 AD   1875 AD

Fig. 6. Chinese lattice design (extracted from [18]).

Table 1. Number of collinear nodes in the design (extracted from [12]).

NCN	1800 AD	1825 AD	1875 AD
2	262	42	0
3	0	84	24
4	0	0	4
5	0	0	6
7	0	0	4
9	0	0	3
11	0	0	2
13	0	8	5
15	0	7	0
17	0	0	4

The (white) nodes, additional edges and the overall number of the given method of representation are presented in Table 2c. In the real life the final project consist of many different styles and shapes. We can present such a situation by summing up Chengtu, Szechwan 1800 AD, 1825 AD and Hanchow, Szechwan 1875 AD(see Table 2d).

The analysed examples show that the introduced VG-2 and VG-3 representations have the same or better expressiveness in comparison with Keles's

Table 2. Comparision of representation collinear representations (extracted from [12]).

(a) for Chengtu, Szechwan 1800 AD

representation	Extra nodes	Extra edges	Together	
Keles'2	0	0	429	100,00%
Grasl's	262	524	1215	238,22%
VG-2	0	0	429	100,00%
VG-3	0	0	429	100,00%

(b) for Chengtu, Szechwan 1825 AD

representation	Extra nodes	Extra edges	Together	
Keles'2	0	1249	1890	100,00%
Grasl's	141	545	1327	70,21%
VG-2	15	293	949	50,21%
VG-3	15	293	949	50,21%

(c) for Hanchow, Szechwan 1875 AD

representation	Extra nodes	Extra edges	Together	
Keles'2	0	1116	1557	100,00%
Grasl's	52	328	821	52,73%
VG-2	28	280	749	48,11%
VG-3	24	276	741	47,59%

(d) for sum of all

representation	Extra nodes	Extra edges	Together	
Keles'2	0	2365	3876	100,00%
Grasl's	455	1397	3363	86,76%
VG-2	43	573	2127	54,88%
VG-3	39	569	2119	54,67%

approach; their advantage grows when longer collinear segments appear in the shape. They are always better than Grasl's approach. The VG-3 representation seems to be slightly better, but the implementation of splitting one of the collinear segments becomes more complex. Thus, we will sketch the solution for VG-2. That proves that introduced VG-2 and VG-3 representations are the most efficient ones.

4 Application of VG-X Notation to Shape Transformation Rules

During definition of a shape grammar, we have to define what kinds of the basic elements can be used as building blocks for shapes generated by the grammar. Three problems have to be solved in real application of the mentioned VG-x representation in 3D design:

- efficiency of dual representation for short and long lines,
- approximation of the final 3D shape by set of planes,
- using as a basic shapes more complicated shapes then designated by set of segments eg. part of circle.

Two last problems appears also in the context Kelly's or Grasl's representation.

4.1 Efficiency of Dual Representation for Short and Long Lines

For graph transformation system there is no problem to use the both representations of collinearity in the same system. The left side of the transformation rule lhs will use the Grasl's collinearity representation. While searching the subgraph of the entire graph G that is isomorphic to lhs, we will convert:

– Keles's in-line edge (black line) and the (only) node connected with the in-line endnodes with direct edges (dashed one)—into four nodes in Grasl's representation (see Fig. 7a),
– direct edges that are not considered in the previous in-line relation—into three nodes in Grasl's representation (see Fig. 7b).

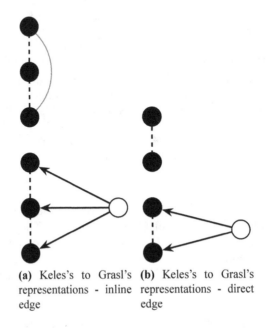

(a) Keles's to Grasl's representations - inline edge (b) Keles's to Grasl's representations - direct edge

Fig. 7. Online conversion (extracted from [12]).

The opposite transformation will be performed after the application of the transformation rule – all the white nodes that participate in this rule and do not point to at least three black nodes are converted to the Grasl's notation.

4.2   Approximation of the Final 3D Shape by Set of Planes

The verification of the segments interdependence is very important in case of 3D representation. Lets consider the segment $\underline{A_1, A_k}$ and segment $\underline{B_1, B_k}$

– if line constains of segments $\underline{A_1, A_k}$ and $\underline{B_1, B_k}$ are intersected or parallel then exist the plane that covers a quadrilateral $<A_1, A_k, B_k, B_1>$
– otherwise we have to represent the shape as the series of tringles: $<A_i, A_{i+1}, B_{i+1}>$ for $i = 1 \ldots k - 1$ and $<A_i, B_{i+1}, B_i>$ for $i = 1 \ldots k - 1$ as presented below.

The second problem is that line intersection can be designated too far from the considered object (outside the designing scope). This problem can be solved as follows:

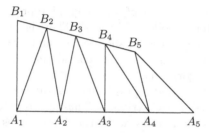

- in an analitical way we designate virtual nodes i.e. such that are not visualized directly,
- this virtual nodes are used for verification of existence and designation proper planes.

In Sect. 4.1 the automatic conversion, by the graph transformation rules has been presented. The easiness of definition the transformation rules basing on different formal representations is also useful here; we can examine the intersection of the lines containing the segments either by finding node that belongs to both collinear sequences covering segments endpoints or in a analytical way. Parallelism can be verified only in an analytical way.

4.3   More Complicated Shapes

In the Virtual Gaudi project [12] we assume that we will describe the shape as Beziér curves (linear, quadratic, cubic or higher order) connected by common nodes. Bezier curve will be denoted by $S^{A_n}(x, y)$, where x and y are the nodes representing end points, and A_n is a set of other $(n-2)$ attributes defining the Bezier curve of the order n. For two curves, we denote $S^{A_n}(x, y) \subset S^{A_n}(w, z)$ if all points of the first curve belong to the second one. For a given n and a set of attributes A_n, we will say that two shapes, are co-n-bezier shapes (denoted $\leftrightarrow$) as if the following conditions are met: for any nodes x, y, u, w, v, z:

- $S^{A_n}(x, y) \leftrightarrow S^{A_n}(u, z)$ if $S^{A_n}(x, y) \subset S^{A_n}(u, z)$
- $\leftrightarrow$ relation is closed under symmetry i.e.
  $S^{A_n}(x, y) \leftrightarrow S^{A_n}(u, z) \Rightarrow S^{A_n}(u, z) \leftrightarrow S^{A_n}(x, y)$
- $\leftrightarrow$ relation is closed under transitivity i.e.
  $S^{A_n}(x, y) \leftrightarrow S^{A_n}(u, w)$ and $S^{A_n}(u, w) \leftrightarrow S^{A_n}(v, z) \Rightarrow S^{A_n}(x, y) \leftrightarrow S^{A_n}(v, z)$

The $S^{A_n}(x, y)$ that does not contain any curves $\leftrightarrow$ related with them will be called minimal and its end nodes will be connected with direct edges.

The shapes grammars use hybrid notation:

- for the presentation layer, the mentioned basic shapes are used to express the designed item,
- for efficient generation of this item, a more complex graph-based representation (based on graph transformation rules) is used.

Here, we compare the efficiency of several graph representations according to the number of source items (nodes and edges). There is a necessity to remember the information about the generated shapes; the number of nodes and edges in the graph are the basic parameters while considering the computational complexity of graph-based algorithms.

Let us note that in $S^{A_n}(x, y)$ representation of the Bezier curves we separate the notation of end nodes and A attributes. Thus, in the graph representation we will represent only these end nodes, while the A attributes will be remembered either as attributes of the edge representing shapes (in case of Keles' approach) or as attributes of the node representing shapes (according to Grasl). The advantage of such a representation is that it is the same for all orders of Bezier curves. For the simplicity of presentation, we will illustrate the mentioned representation based on the co-1-bezier shape called line segments (shortened to $S(x, y)$) and collinear shape relation.

5   Conclusions

The more compact graph representation of the shapes generated by shape grammars is very important, as the efficiency of graph transformation algorithms depends on the graph size (number of nodes and edges). In this context, efficient representation of the collinear segments has been proposed in [12]. Basing on the presented representation for 2D shapes its extension for 3D shape representation has been examined. The importance of efficient collinearity representation grows because approximation of the shape covering two non-itersected or non-parallel segments is made by series of triangles (see Sect. 4.2). The necessity of splitting these segments introduce new collinear points that has to be represented; their number grows with increasing accuracy of approximation. The second problem is with the verification of the segments intersection and parallelism; here we sometimes have to consider virtual nodes (that represent object located outside the designing scope) that are designated and verified in an analytical way.

The definition of transformation rule application, extended by the conversion mechanisms, that allows us to combine two different representations of the collinear segments, has been presented in [12]. Here this mechanism has been extended by the application transformation rules for verification of line intersection or parallelism.

It should also be noted that the mentioned approach can be extended to representation of co-n-bezier shapes (defined in Sect. 4), which is important in real-world application of shape grammars, and it could by also apply in 3D space by application of the method proposed by [6].

Acknowledgements. This work has been partially supported by AGH UST research project 11.11.120.859.

References

1. Agarwal, M., Cagan, J., Stiny, G.: A micro language: generating MEMS resonators by using a coupled form-function shape grammar. Environ. Plan. B: Plan. Des. **27**(4), 615–626 (2000). https://doi.org/10.1068/b2619
2. Beirão, J.: CityMaker designing grammars for urban design. Architecture and the Built Environment (2012)
3. Duarte, J.P.: Towards the mass customization of housing: the grammar of Siza's houses at Malagueira. Environ. Plan. B: Plan. Des. **32**(3), 347–380 (2005). https://doi.org/10.1068/b31124
4. Flasinski, M.: Distorted pattern analysis with the help of node label controlled graph languages. Pattern Recognit. **23**(7), 765–774 (1990). https://doi.org/10.1016/0031-3203(90)90099-7
5. Grasl, T., Economou, A.: GRAPE: using graph grammars to implement shape grammars. In: Proceedings of the 2011 Symposium on Simulation for Architecture and Urban Design, Boston, Massachusetts, pp. 21–28. SCITEPRESS (2011)
6. Faraway, J.J., Reed, M.P., Wang, J.: Modelling three-dimensional trajectories by using Bézier curves with application to hand motion. J. R. Stat. Soc.: Ser. C (Appl. Stat.) **56**(5), 571–585 (2007). https://rss.onlinelibrary.wiley.com/doi/abs/10.1111/j.1467-9876.2007.00592.x
7. McCormack, J.P., Cagan, J., Vogel, C.M.: Speaking the Buick language: capturing, understanding, and exploring brand identity with shape grammars. Des. Stud. **25**, 1–29 (2004)
8. Keles, H.Y., Özkar, M., Tari, S.: Embedding shapes without predefined parts. Environ. Plan. B: Plan. Des. **37**(4), 664–681 (2010). https://doi.org/10.1068/b36010
9. Knight, T., Stiny, G.: Making grammars: from computing with shapes to computing with things. Des. Stud. **41**, 8–28 (2015)
10. Knight, T.W.: Transformations of De Stijl art: the paintings of Georges Vantongerloo and Fritz Glarner. Environ. Plan. B: Plan. Des. **16**(1), 51–98 (1989). https://doi.org/10.1068/b160051
11. Knight, T.: Shape grammars in education and practice: histrory and prospects. Int. J. Des. Comput. **2** (1999)
12. Kotulska, K., Kotulski, L.: On the efficient graph representation of collinear relation in the shape grammars. In: Proceedings of the International Conference on Computer-Human Interaction Research and Applications - Volume 1: CHIRA, pp. 60–66. INSTICC, SciTePress (2017)
13. Kotulski, L., Sedziwy, A.: GRADIS - the multiagent environment supported by graph transformations. Simul. Model. Pract. Theory **18**(10), 1515–1525 (2010). https://doi.org/10.1016/j.simpat.2010.05.013
14. Krzysztof Lukaszczyk, P.G.: Modeling of Antonio Gaudi's architectural objects with the usage of shape grammars. Master's thesis, EAIiB AGH UST, Poland (2010)
15. Müller, P., Wonka, P., Haegler, S., Ulmer, A., Van Gool, L.: Procedural modeling of buildings. ACM Trans. Graph. **25**(3), 614–623 (2006). https://doi.org/10.1145/1141911.1141931
16. Muslimin, R.: Interweaving grammar: reconfiguring vernacular structure through parametric shape grammar. Int. J. Arch. Comput. **8**(2), 93–110 (2010). https://doi.org/10.1260/1478-0771.8.2.93
17. Stiny, G.: Shape: Talking About Seeing and Doing. The MIT Press, Cambridge (2006)

18. Stiny, G.: Ice-ray: a note on the generation of chinese lattice designs. Environ. Plan. B **4**, 89–98 (1977)
19. Stiny, G.: Introduction to shape and shape grammars. Environ. Plan. **7**(7), 343–351 (1980)
20. Stiny, G., Mitchell, W.J.: The grammar of paradise: on the generation of Mughul gardens. Environ. Plan. B: Plan. Des. **7**(2), 209–226 (1980). https://doi.org/10.1068/b070209
21. Stiny, G., Gips, J.: Shape grammars and the generative specification of painting and sculpture. In: IFIP Congress (2), pp. 1460–1465 (1971)

Distinct Sources of a Bovine Blastocyst Digital Image Do not Produce the Same Classification by a Previously Trained Software Using Artificial Neural Network

Vitória Bertogna Guilherme[1], Micheli Pronunciate[2],
Priscila Helena dos Santos[1], Diego de Souza Ciniciato[3],
Maria Beatriz Takahashi[3], José Celso Rocha[3],
and Marcelo Fábio Gouveia Nogueira[1,2(✉)]

[1] Laboratório de Micromanipulação Embrionária,
School of Sciences and Languages, Universidade Estadual Paulista (Unesp),
Av. Dom Antonio 2100, Assis, Brazil
marcelo.fabio@unesp.br
[2] Laboratório Multiusuário FitoFarmaTec, Institute of Biosciences,
Unesp, Rubião Jr., Botucatu, Brazil
[3] Laboratório de Matemática Aplicada, School of Sciences and Languages,
Unesp, Av. Dom Antonio 2100, Assis, Brazil

Abstract. We develop an online graphical and intuitive interface connected to a server aiming to facilitate access to professionals worldwide that face problems with bovine blastocysts classification. The interface Blasto3Q (3Q is referred to the three qualities of the blastocyst grading) contains a description of 24 variables that are extracted from the image of the blastocyst and analyzed by three Artificial Neural Networks (ANNs) that classifies the same loaded image. The same embryo (*i.e.*, the biological specimen) was submitted to digital image capture by the control group (inverted microscope with 40x of magnification) and to experimental group (stereomicroscope with maximum of magnification plus 4x zoom from the cell phone). The 36 images obtained from control and experimental groups were uploaded on the Blasto3Q. Each image from both sources was evaluated for segmentation and submitted (only if it could be properly or partially segmented) to the quality grade classification by the three ANNs of the Blasto3Q program. In the group control, all the images were properly segmented, whereas 38.9% (07/18) and 61.1% (11/18) of the images from the experimental group, respectively could not be segmented or were partially segmented. The percentage of agreement was calculated when the same blastocyst was evaluated by the same ANN from the two sources (control and experimental groups). On the 54 potential evaluations of the three ANNs (*i.e.*, 18 images been evaluated by the three networks) from the experimental group only 22.2% agreed with evaluations of the control (12/54). Of the remaining 42 disagreed evaluations from experimental group, 21 were unable to be performed and 21 were wrongly processed when compared with control evaluation.

V. B. Guilherme, M. Pronunciate and P. H. dos Santos—Authors contributed equally to the study.

A. Holzinger et al. (Eds.): CHIRA 2017, CCIS 654, pp. 139–153, 2019.
https://doi.org/10.1007/978-3-030-32965-5_8

1 Introduction

Brazil is the largest beef exporter in the world with a cattle herd of 218.2 million of animals [1], number that is superior of the Brazilian population (207 million at 2017) [2]. This production is the major economic activity of country, moved US\$ 5.3 billion at 2016 and employed 1.6 million people. It is also the major producer of *in vitro* bovine embryos, with 366.517 embryos/year, that is around 70% of the world production [3]. The Brazilian program of *in vitro* production (IVP) of bovine embryos started on 1990, but the first three births only occurred in 1994. This achievement used Nellore breed immature oocytes, frozen-thawed semen and culture system. Currently, the IVP is used commercially for several laboratories to research and multiplication of genetic material in the animal production [4]. This production has utmost importance for international and national improvement in cattle genetics and productivity.

The animal production has undergone many changes in the last 50 years, due to a livestock sector and agricultural research. In this case, the development of *in vitro* techniques for production of cattle embryos has proved to be useful. The production of bovine embryos for commercial purposes follows the steps: they are produced *in vitro* and transferred to synchronized receptors when they reach the blastocyst stage [5].

To their production, the donor cow undergoes a system called *ovum*-pick up to retrieve its oocytes (commercial purpose) or the ovarian follicles could be aspirated on ovaries from abattoir (research purpose) [5].

On contrary to the IVP system, there is a more natural way to produce bovine embryos that is the multiple ovulation and embryo transfer (MOET). It is a treatment used to increase the number of ovulations higher than the average for the species using a sort of hormones and lasting up to 9–10 days [5]. Six to eight days after the artificial insemination of the superstimulated cows in MOET, the embryo presumptively has reach the uterus. In this stage, the embryos are still surrounded by the *zona pellucida* and are tolerant to some handling out of the cow body. Although both *in vitro* (IVP) and *in vivo* (MOET) produced embryos are tolerant, its degree is dependent from the original environment (*in vivo* or *in vitro*) whether them were derived and mainly by their quality [5].

There is some difference between embryos derived from IVP or MOET. The embryos produced *in vivo* have round shape, brownish colour, plasmatic membranes of the blastocysts closely to the *zona pellucida*, and the inner cell mass (ICM) is surrounded by small intercellular spaces [6, 7]. The embryos produced *in vitro* generally are darker (this has been associated with a higher accumulation of lipid or lipid like granules in the cytoplasm due to the use of serum in the culture medium) [8]. Blastomeres of *in vitro* embryos appear more swollen, the perivitelline space is smaller at all pre-compaction stages [8], have a decreased cell count [9] and an increased number of vacuoles in comparison to those *in vivo* produced [10, 11].

1.1 Classification of Embryos by Morphological Analysis

The embryonic quality is determinate based on the number and appearance of cells. This classification follows the International Embryo Transfer Society (IETS) [12], using two codes of description, that is, one to assign the quality and the other to the stage of development. The standard evaluation is performed with a stereomicroscope at 50 to 100X magnification. The diameter of bovine embryo is 120 to 190 μm, including the *zona pellucida* (12 to 15 μm). The ideal embryo is compact and spherical with blastomeres of similar size, color and texture uniforms; cytoplasm cannot be granular or vesiculated. The periviteline space should be clear and the *zona pellucida* uniform not cracked or collapsed. The code for the stage of development is numeric, varying from "1" to unfertilized oocyte or 1-cell embryo, to "9" for expanding hatched blastocyst. The code for quality is based on the morphological integrity of embryos, and it is also ranging from "1" (to good or excellent), when they have symmetrical and spherical mass, the cellular material is at 85% intact and irregularities are relatively minor; "2" (to fair) when the embryos have moderate irregularities in the overall shape of embryonic mass or size and color; "3" (to poor) when major irregularities in shape or other parameters are observed; and "4" (to dead or degenerating embryos) that is, a non-viable structure.

Despite this classification, to evaluate bovine embryos is directly affected by the embryologist's accuracy, experience and mood [13]. The reason for this interference is that the morphological analysis does not measure any objective variables to determine the embryo classification. The reason is that the human vision is subjectively being able to extract numerous information of an image but ignoring some kinds or not observing another one and it is based on a comparison among objects or images. Every time our eyes are like a tool to analysis results of experiments, but when we have to analyze an image, there is a difficulty of at judging color or brightness of shapes and features [14]. Thus the analyses by an embryologist may have low reproducibility [15]. Farin *et al.* [16] described two kinds of error by embryologist that support that affirmation. First is the inter-evaluator error, when the same embryo can be classified with different quality grades by different embryologists or (intra-evaluator error) when the same embryologist classifies the same embryo in different grades. This could specially to occur when the quality grade is borderline, the evaluator is inexperience, he is tired, or his mood is altered. Due all the reasons already mentioned, the embryo evaluation is less reproducible and objective as desired. However, it is one of the most critical steps of the embryo transfer procedure (IVP or MOET) and has a strong relation to a successful pregnancy establishment [12].

1.2   The Semi-automatized Methods to Evaluate the Embryo Quality

Therefore, several methods have been or are being developed to improve the process of embryo classification that has not external effects. Many embryologists select the oocytes/embryos by a non-invasive examination based on simple observation focused on morphology and kinetics of their developmental stage (third day of culture or blastocyst stage) [17]. Among then, embryo metabolism analysis, cellular respiration measurement, evaluation by time-lapse video [18], the quality on *in vitro* growth of embryos, the integrity of blastomeres membrane [18, reviewed by 19, 20] and electron-microscopy analysis [18, reviewed by 21]. Other kinds of evaluation have been used in attempt of find a better solution to classify the embryo quality. As example, Melo *et al.* [22] described an automatic segmentation procedure of bovine embryos, without the use of Artificial Intelligence (AI) and whose proposal was calculated the sensitivity, specificity and accuracy's method. The database used in this work was made up of 30 histological slides (staining with Sudan Black B) in different stage of development: early cleavage, morula and blastocyst and, the image was acquired by inverted light microscope Olympus IX71 with digital camera coupled (Lumenera Infinity 1-1). Each slide was photographed at a magnification of 100x, using 10x objective lens and ocular lens. Although the positive results and the high rates of sensitivity and specificity it is not applicable to the bovine embryos yet.

Time-lapse is a non-invasive technology mainly used to human embryos to measure morphokinetic parameters such as the timing of karyogamy, time intervals between cytokinesis and its abnormal events that results in uneven blastomeres size [23, 24]. With this technology, the embryos can monitored without removing them from the incubator as in another morphological and dynamics analysis. Images are made by a camera inbuilt the incubator that capture images of the embryos at timed intervals [reviewed by 18, 25]. Among the current time-lapse systems, two are the most widely used technologies: the Embryoscope/Fertilitech (an incubator with an integrate time-lapse system) [26, 27] and the Primo Vision/Vitrolife (a compact digital inverted microscope system) [26, 27] and, both use bright field technology.

Other kind of analysis of embryo quality is the semi-automatized grading method of human blastocyst using a support vector machine. It performs the classification by determining a separation rule between two sets of feature values (support vectors) [28]. Among 17 classification methods tested by Meyer [29], this produced the best performance.

From photographs of oocyte and embryos at the 4-cells stage, Manna *et al.* [17] used AI techniques that are based on (*i*) segmentation (selection of the correct region of interest in the image) and pre-processing for reducing artefacts due to noise, blur or illumination conditions; (*ii*) feature extraction (it is usually dependent of numerical descriptors) that represent in a compact way the starting image (such as LBP) [17, 18, 30]; and (*iii*) definition of a classification system, in which the classifier is trained using the data stored in the knowledge base.

Several authors proposed the use of mathematical and statistic tools for the evaluation of the embryo quality, like the multivariate logistic regression with eight predictive factors for the classification of embryos according to implantation potential [18, 31], computer-assisted scoring system (CASS) [18, 32] that is supposed to have a higher discriminatory power for embryo selection, over the standard scoring system that has intrinsic examiner variability. It was also used the multivariate logistic regression (LR) system together with multivariate adaptive regression splines (MARS) that had shown improvement on predictive model when using the computer assisted scoring system associated with data mining. Nevertheless, any of these methods were totally effective in the prediction and the morphological analysis still is widely used to evaluate the embryo quality [18, reviewed by 33].

1.3   The Artificial Intelligence Technique

The Artificial Intelligence (AI) is the technique that has potential to develop objective, reproducible and non-invasive methodology to predict embryo quality with high levels of accuracy [18]. A specific method as artificial neural network (ANN) along with genetic algorithm (GA) could be used to simulate an accuracy predictive model [34]. ANNs are inspired by the early models of sensory processing by the brain that has a highest and interconnecting neurons network and communicate by electric surge (through axons, synapse and dendrites). An ANN can be creating using a model of neural network in a computer. Applying algorithms that imitate neurons real process we can make the network learn to solve problems. This is make of interactive way presenting examples with known classification, one before other (it is called learning or training) [35]. GA is a search and optimization method inspired by genetic mechanisms under natural evolution [18, 36], whilst the ANN is a technique based on how human neurons transmit and process information to learn and it is indicated for the resolution of complex and nonlinear problems. Once properly trained, the ANN is capable to perform prediction from new data which it has never had access [37, 38]. It was first proposed for mouse embryo (*in vivo* produced) and posteriorly to *in vitro* produced bovine blastocyst but comprising the stages between the initial and expansion [18; reviewed by 39, 40].

Supported by the GA, three ANNs (with the best accuracy) were developed after to have been trained to classify bovine blastocyst images based on the IETS standards [41, 42]. In that study, 482 blastocyst images dataset were used to train some ANNs, from which the best obtained 76.4% of accuracy. Three experienced embryologists from the major Brazilian and world leader company (*In Vitro Brazil*, Mogi Mirim, São Paulo state, Brazil) were responsible to previously evaluate the embryo quality (according IETS standards) to support the ANN learning.

1.4 The Blasto3Q Algorithm

The work mentioned above, resulted in two different interfaces, one using the MATLAB® platform and an interface using multiplatform approach for online purpose. Both of them, we called "Blasto3Q" program (3Q is refer to the three qualities of blastocysts evaluation) [41, 42]. In the first case, the interface created (in accordance with the recommendations for the commercial use of the program) allows the user interact with the program in a fast and intuitive way. This interface contains a description of the 24 variables that are extracted from the image and analyzed by the ANNs that classifies the same loaded image through the best three obtained ANNs. The second developed interface allows the on-line use of Blasto3Q via a cell phone (smartphone) or PC.

1.4.1 The Process to Image Acquire

Using MATLAB platform, it was possible the automatized analysis without the embryologist's intervention. For standardization, the software consecutively followed the steps of image import (BMP or JPG), conversion to greyscale (8-bit greyscale), resolution and proportion adjustment (we choose 640 × 480 pixels as the default resolution because it is the lowest standard and provides sufficient information for interpretation), and intensity adjustment (1% of all information becomes saturated between light and dark pixels; Rocha *et al.* [41, 42]). These steps facilitate the next process, the segmentation.

1.4.2 Image Segmentation

To the image segmentation they were properly isolated from the background and were then subjected to the information extraction techniques. The segmentation algorithm is composed for 4 steps describe below (more details in our previous works) [41, 42]. The first step was calculating the magnitude of the image gradient and the edges were highlighted in all directions, it is important to next steps and essential to characterize the circular shape of the embryo. Following the magnitude gradient, we calculated the binary image and select a value of 128 as intensity threshold. After that, we use the Circular Hough Transform (CHT) to detect the embryo circumference and mapping the image and thus provide an isolated embryo background image [43]. The algorithm search for circles in two stages: first, it searches by circles with radius between 100 and 150 pixels and then, for circles with radius between 150 and 200 pixels to greater accuracy. Therefore, both initial blastocysts (smaller) or expanded blastocysts (larger) can be detected. At the end of both searches, in each image, the detected circle's metrics are compared and the largest radius is used after the best circle is detected. The last step is the blastocyst isolation, where is generated tree versions of the image: (i) the radius of circumference is increase 5 pixels, to make sure that *zona pellucida* is included (called ER); (ii) the radius is decrease by 40 pixel to exclude the trophecto-derm selecting the inner mass cells (IMC) and blastocoel for analysis only (called RR); and (iii) the difference between ER and RR. Therefore, only the trophectoderm region was isolated in the image (called TE). The pixel values, which determined the expansion (ER) and the contraction (RR) of the blastocysts images, were obtained by assessment of the image database.

The image texture was defined by repeated random regular patterns in a region of the image that provided information on the surface structure [41, 44]. It is an important characteristic that is used to identify the regions of interest in an image [45]. The statistical methods used to analysis the textures in images was the grey level co-occurrence matrix (GLCM). Considered the most efficient and describes the spatial distribution of the intensity values of the pixels by considering a determined distance and angle, which makes it possible to recognize and classify textures [44, 46].

1.4.3 Extraction of Variables

After image standardization and segmentation, 36 variables were extracted, sufficient to extract all the relevant information for the representation of the analyzed bovine blastocyst image. For the complete description of variables, see previous work [42]. The collinearity analysis was performed to eliminate those variables that were corre-lated with one another (*i.e.*, redundant). It was also possible to determine the Variance Inflation Factor (VIF; which represents the degree of independent variable multi-collinearity when compared with the other independent variables). Collinear variables can be those with higher VIF values than 10. Thirteen iterations were performed until all the variables had a VIF value of less than or equal to 10. Thus, 24 variables remained for use in the ANN.

For the ANN learning process, the Backpropagation algorithm was used [33]. The total of images (n = 482) was divided into training (70%), validation (15%) and test (15%). The accuracy of the obtained ANN was verified according to the error between the real values (the mode of the embryologists' evaluation) and the values obtained by the ANN [47]. Currently, there is no standard method for obtaining the best architecture (the number of neurons in each layer, number of layers, training and transfer functions) of the ANN for a fittest solution of a problem [41, 48]. Thus, the GA technique was used to improve the efficiency on determining the best ANN architecture.

We considered that the population to be studied by the GA was formed by different ANNs architectures, and the goal was to obtain networks that had the lowest error in the blastocyst image classification.

The GA technique developed in our study considered the creation of an initial ANN population with different architectures (each one is called "individuals"), which was randomly generated and composed of 100, 200 or 300 individuals. Each one was defined by a "genetic code", that is, a specific pattern of 9 different "genes" representing the variables (*i.e.*, the number of neurons in the first, second and third hidden layer; the transfer function for the first, second and third hidden layer; the transfer function for the output layer; the training function to be used; and the number of hidden layers to be used). Each ANN was trained and tested, and their success percentage for the degree of classification was assessed.

This chapter is a continuation of a previous work [41, 49], extending it with new data and aiming the development of a Graphical User Interface to the users that could not purchase or access an inverted microscope to capture digital images. In addition, embryologists from around the word can access the technique online (by the internet), without downloading or installing the software executable. Furthermore, we describe the necessity of smartphone adapters use for stereomicroscope ocular lens to grade blastocysts in a real-time.

2 Methodology

Embryos were produced *in vitro* from *cumulus*-oocytes complex from antral follicles of slaughtered cows based on the protocol previously published [50]. On the day 7 of *in vitro* culture (day 0 was on *in vitro* insemination), the embryos were recovered from the culture. Only the embryos morphologically classified as expanded blastocyst with inner cell mass (ICM) relatively smaller than blastocoele and a thin layer of trophectoderm [12], was utilized to evaluation. First, the expanded blastocysts were separated on phosphate buffered saline (PBS) solution to the caption of image. In the experimental group, the embryo digital image was captured with a Motorola smartphone G4 Plus (ANDROID™ 7.0 system) with 16 megapixels of camera, lens aperture of F/2,0 and digital zoom of 4x through the ocular lens from a Leica stereomicroscope (S8 APO - 10x magnification) with maximum zoom magnification (8x). Different of previous study, it was not necessary the use of an extra macro lens coupled to the smartphone by a clip to capture the images from the stereomicroscope (Fig. 1).

The images were stored in JPG format. Then, images of the same embryos were also acquired by inverted microscope Nikon Eclipse T*i* coupled to a Nikon Digital Sight DSRi1 at 40x magnification in the software NIS Elements Ar 3.0 (control group). The images were stored in JPG format in 8-bit color (RGB) at a resolution of 1280 × 1024 pixel. To the capture of pictures with the smartphone and inverted microscope, the embryos were adjusted in a standardized position with ICM perpendicular to the focal plane (Fig. 2). Each picture contained only one blastocyst and it is important to note that when it came from the smartphone, the embryo occupied a smaller area of the entire image compared with images from the inverted microscope.

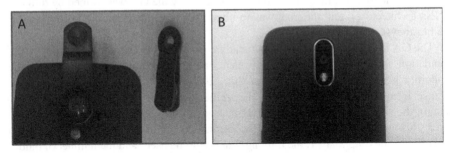

Fig. 1. (A) Macro lens coupled to the smartphone lens by a clip. Its use was proposed in our previous study (Ciniciato *et al.* [49]). (B) In the present work that device was not necessary since there was no difference (in quality or size of the images acquired by the phone) when the smartphone lens was directly juxtaposed to the stereomicroscope ocular lens.

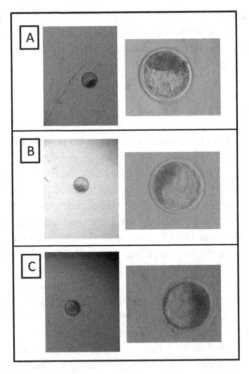

Fig. 2. Illustrative samples of the images captured by the smartphone without macro lens (left column) and with the inverted microscope (right column), from three different embryos (lines A, B and C). When the smartphone was used, the embryos occupied a smaller area of the image in comparison to the inverted microscope image.

Embryos from phone images occupied on average 3.01% of total area of the image and their diameter was intercepted, on average, by 21.57% of a line from the extreme points at the largest width of the image (ImageJ; https://imagej.nih.gov/ij/index.html). In control group, the embryos had an average occupation of 26.95% of total area of they were intercepted on average by 49.61% on the maximum width.

To analyze the acquired images, was used the desktop version of Blasto3Q software. First, the image was uploaded on the program, so the image was processed and evaluated by the already trained algorithm Blasto3Q, which is detailed described in [42]. In the software, the uploaded images underwent an automatized segmentation process, whereby the images were properly isolated from the background. The image could be fully, partially or non-segmented (Fig. 3). To have a reliable result (*i.e.*, a classification by Blasto3Q), numerical variables should be extracted from the image. Once non-segmented images did not produce those variables, only the images that were properly or partially segmented were considered to the comparison of evaluation performance.

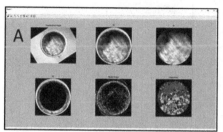 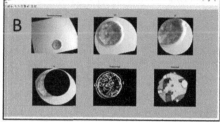

Fig. 3. Comparison between perfect (A) and partial segmentation (B) of a blastocyst image. All the images from control group produced a perfect segmentation, whereas in the experimental group there was no perfect segmentation at all images processed.

After the segmentation, the images were submitted to quality grade classification of the three ANNs of the Blasto3Q program to a comparison through the software. For this, one of the ANNs is selected by bottoms at the graphic user interface to analyze the uploaded image. Each ANN deliveries only one quality grade to the user, that is, poor, fair or excellent/good. The output of the same ANN sometimes differed from the same embryo when the sources (control or experimental groups) were different (Fig. 4).

3 Results

Eighteen *in vitro* produced blastocysts were used to obtain distinct images (two biological replicates were performed with 11 and 07 embryos). The same embryo was submitted to digital image capture by the control group (inverted microscope with 40x of magnification) and to experimental group (stereomicroscope with maximum of magnification [80x] plus 4x zoom from the cell phone). The 36 images obtained from control and experimental groups were uploaded on the program Blasto3Q (from an executable file).

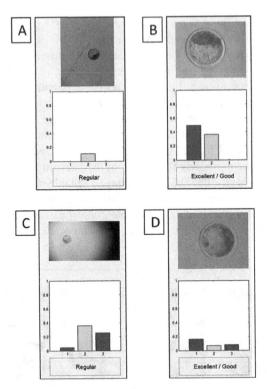

Fig. 4. Illustrative samples of the result showed in the graphic user interface (GUI) of Blasto3Q. The GUI shows the uploaded image (raw image) and the classification done by one of the chosen ANNs. Images A and B are from the same embryo when the image was captured by a smartphone (A) and an inverted microscope (B). Images C (smartphone capture) and D (inverted microscope capture) are both from another embryo. The GUI differed between the sources (group) regarding to the showed classification, yet the embryo was the same. The colored bars in the GUI above numbers 1, 2 and 3 - and meaning the quality grades (excellent/good, fair, and poor, respectively) - allow a visual conclusion of what was the higher value (*i.e.*, the highest bar is the quality grade classification).

Each image from both sources was evaluated for segmentation (*i.e.*, the proper isolation of the embryo and of its parts) since that isolation is a prerequisite to the program obtain numerical values from segmented parts of the image. All images from control group were properly segmented (as showed in the Fig. 3A) whereas none image was in the experimental group. In this, 38.9% of the images (07/18) could not be segmented at all, thus no numerical variables were extracted from the images and no quality grade of the embryo could be evaluated by the Blasto3Q. Eleven images from experimental group (61.1%; 11/18) were partially segmented, *i.e.* although the embryo was isolated and numerical values could be extracted there was a mismatch and some parts of the embryo were lost during segmentation steps (as exemplified in the Fig. 3B).

The 11 blastocyst images segmented properly (control group) or partially (experimental group) were submitted to the quality grade classification by the three artificial neural networks (ANNs) of the Blasto3Q program. It is mean that each of the image was evaluated by three different networks providing 33 quality grades for control and experimental groups. The percentage of agreement was calculated between the same blastocyst been evaluated by the same artificial neural network from the two sources (control and experimental groups). A total of 36.4% of agreement (12/33) was obtained by ANNs 1, 2 and 3 (3, 4 and 5 of agreement, respectively). The disagreement (63.6%; 21/33) between the groups were 8, 7 and 6 respectively for ANNs 1, 2 and 3.

Overall, from the 54 potential evaluations of the three ANNs from the 18 images of the experimental group, only 22.2% were concordant with the control (12/54). The remaining 42 evaluations were unable to be performed (21) or were wrongly processed (21).

4   Discussion

The alternative source of image capture (from a smartphone) produced a kind of embryo characterization that impaired the Blasto3Q program to properly classify it. It was notorious by the fully segmentation criterion. Since the program was trained with the higher percentage and interception of the embryo image covering the total area of the picture (from an inverted microscope capture) and, consequently, with a higher diameter of the embryo in the image to be recognizable by the segmentation process. We assume that the total failure from the 18 images (experimental group) to be properly segmented was due the smaller area and interception of the embryo image into the total picture uploaded.

As ANN is based on the machine learning concept, the Blasto3Q algorithm learned to classify blastocyst from the pattern observed in the inverted microscope capture. In this way, the 76% accuracy obtained in its training was lost because the evaluation is based from the numerical values extracted of the segmented image. As observed, none image could be fully segmented and only 61.1% were partially segmented in the experimental group. The numerical variables extracted from partially segmentation surely produced a mismatch to the real information contained in the full embryo image. In this way, the bad quality variables extracted (experimental group) were unable to pair the quality evaluation from control group, with only 36.4% of agreed classification between them.

We did not test it, but our hypothesis is that a simple readjustment of the *radius* size to search for the embryo (adjusted for a higher *radius* in the program Blasto3Q, since it was based entirely from inverted microscope images) could improve or even repair the fault observed in this work. The *radius* size is a parameter used by Hough transform to find a circularity in the total image and it is the way to segment only the embryo (by its almost perfect and constant circularity).

The other inferred possibility to correct the error, could be the full re-training of the algorithm and, in this time, with a full database composed only by smartphone blastocyst pictures. Maybe the association of a new phone image database and resizing the radius of the embryo could properly fit the algorithm Blasto3Q to the alternative use of smartphones as the tool to directly capture images from stereomicroscope.

5 Conclusion

We concluded that, with the current training of the Blasto3Q algorithm, it was not possible the use of a smartphone camera to directly capture blastocyst images from the stereomicroscope ocular lens. The agreement rate of the embryo classification between the standard and the alternative proposal was too low (22.2%) to be considered feasible.

Acknowledgement. The author's research is supported by grants #2012/50533-2, 2013-05083-1, 2006/06491-2, 2011/06179-7, 2012/20110-2 and 2016/19004-4 from São Paulo Research Foundation (FAPESP). We also thank Agência UNESP de Inovação (AUIN) for processing the national and international patents of the invention.

References

1. Instituto Brasileiro de Geografia e Estatística IBGE: Produção Pecuária Municipal 2016. IBGE 44, 14 (2016). E-book https://biblioteca.ibge.gov.br/visualizacao/periodicos/84/ppm_2016v44br.pdf
2. Instituto Brasileiro de Geografia e Estatística IBGE. Diretoria de Pesquisas – DPE: Coordenação de População e Indicadores Sociais - COPIS. Digital doc. 1 (2017). ftp://ftp.ibge.gov.br/Estimativas_de_Populacao/Estimativas_2017/estimativa_dou_2017.pdf
3. Ereno, D.: Marcadores da Fertilização: Novas técnicas mapeiam a função de proteínas, carboidratos e lipídeos para obtenção de embriões bovinos de melhor qualidade. Tecnologia Pecuária, Revista FAPESP. e-book, 62 (2015). http://revistapesquisa.fapesp.br/wp-content/uploads/2015/05/062-067_embriao-bovino_231.pdf
4. Mello, R.R.C.: In vitro embryo production in cattle. Rev. Bras. Reprod. Anim. 40(2), 58–64 (2016)
5. Hyttel, P., Sinowatz, F., Vejsted, M., et al.: Essential of Domestic Animal Embryology. Sauders/Elsevier, Edinburgh (2010)
6. Fair, T., Lonergan, P., Dinnyes, A., Cottel, D.C., Hyttel, P., et al.: Ultrastructure of bovine blastocysts following cryopreservation: effect of method of blastocyst production. Mol. Reprod. Dev. 58, 186–195 (2001). https://doi.org/10.1002/1098-2795(200102)58:2%3C186:AID-MRD8%3E3.0.CO;2-N
7. Rizos, D., Fair, T., Papadopoulos, S., Boland, M.P., Lonergan, P.: Developmental, qualitative, and ultrastructural differences between ovine and bovine embryos produced in vivo or in vitro. Mol. Reprod. Dev. 62, 320–327 (2002). https://doi.org/10.1002/mrd.10138
8. Holm, P., Callesen, H.: In vivo versus in vitro produced bovine ova: similarities and differences relevant for practical application. Reprod. Nutr. Dev. 38(6), 579–594 (1998)
9. Camargo, L.S.A., Viana, J.H.M., Sá, W.F., Ferreira, F.M., Ramos, A.A., et al.: Factors influencing in vitro embryo production. Anim. Reprod. 3(1), 19–28 (2006)
10. Crosier, A.E., Farin, P.W., Dykstra, M.J., Alexander, J.E., Farin, C.E.: Ultrastructural morphometry of bovine blastocysts produced in vivo or in vitro. Biol. Reprod. 64, 1375–1385 (2001)
11. Dode, M.A.N., Leme, L.O., Sprícigo, L.F.W.: Cryopreservation of in vitro produced bovine embryos. Rev. Bras. Repro. Anim. 37(2), 145–150 (2013)

12. Bó, G., Mapletoft, R.: Evaluation and classification of bovine embryos. Anim. Reprod. **54**, 344–348 (2013)
13. Lindner, G., Wright, R.W.J.: Bovine embryo morphology and avaluation. Theriogenology **20**, 407–416 (1983). https://doi.org/10.1016/0093-691X(83)90201-7
14. Russ, J.C.: The Image Processing Handbook, 5th edn. CRC Press, Boca Raton (2008)
15. Bényei, B., Komlósi, I., Pécsi, A., Pollott, G., Marcos, C.H., et al.: The effect of internal and external factors on bovine embryo transfer results in a tropical environment. Anim. Reprod. Sci. **93**, 268–279 (2006). https://doi.org/10.1016/j.anireprosci.2005.07.012
16. Farin, P.W., Britt, J.H., Shaw, D.W., Slenning, B.D.: Agreement among evaluators of bovine embryos produced in vivo or in vitro. Theriogenology **95**, 339–349 (1995). https://doi.org/10.1016/0093-691X(95)00189-F
17. Manna, C., Nanni, L., Lumini, A., Pappalardo, S.: Artificial intelligence techniques for embryo and oocyte classification. Reprod. Biomed. Online **26**, 42–49 (2013). https://doi.org/10.1016/j.rbmo.2012.09.015
18. Rocha, J.C., Passalia, F., Matos, F.D., Maserati Jr., M.P., Alves, M.F., et al.: Methods for assessing the quality of mammalian embryos: how far we are from the gold standard? JBRA Assist. Reprod. **20**(3), 150–158 (2016). https://doi.org/10.5935/1518-0557.20160033
19. Hoshi, H.: In vitro production of bovine embryos and their application for embryo transfer. Thereogenology **59**, 675–685 (2003). https://doi.org/10.1016/S0093-691X(02)01247-5
20. Held, E., Mertens, E.M., Mohammadi-Sangcheshmeh, A.M., Salilew-Wondim, D., Bessen-felder, U., et al.: Zona pellucida birefringence correlates with developmental capacity of bovine oocytes classified by maturational environment, COC morphology and G6PDH activity. Reprod. Fert. Dev. **24**, 568–579 (2012). https://doi.org/10.1071/RD11112
21. López-Damiám, E.P., Galina, C.S., Merchant, H., Cedilo-Peláez, C., Aspron, M.: Assessment of Bos taurus embryos comparing stereoscopyc microscopy and transmission eléctron microscopy. J. Cell Anim. Biol. **2**, 72–78 (2008)
22. Melo, D.H., Nascimento, M.Z., Oliveira, D.L., Neves, L.A., Annes, K.: Algorithms for automatic segmentation of bovine embryos produced in vitro. J. Phys: Conf. Ser. **490**, 121–125 (2014). https://doi.org/10.1088/1742-6595/490/1/012125
23. Wong, C., Chen, A.A., Behr, B., Shen, S.: Time-lapse microscopy and image analysis in basic and clinical embryo development research. Reprod. Biomed. Online **26**, 120–129 (2013). https://doi.org/10.1016/j.rbmo.2012.11.003
24. Sutton-McDowall, M.L., Gosnell, M., Anwer, A.G., White, M., Purdey, M.: Hyperspectral microscopy can detect metabolic heterogeneity within bovine post-compaction embryos incubated under two oxygen concentrations (7% versus 20%). Hum. Reprod. **32**(10), 2016–2025 (2017). https://doi.org/10.1093/humrep/dex261
25. Kovacs, P.: Embryos selection: the role of time-lapse monitoring. Reprod. Biol. Endocrinol. **12**, 124 (2014). https://doi.org/10.1186/1477-7827-12-124
26. Montag, M., Toth, B., Strowitzki, T.: New approaches to embryo selection. Reprod. Biomed. Online **27**, 539–546 (2013). https://doi.org/10.1016/j.rbmo.2013.05.013
27. VerMilyea, M.D., Tanb, L., Anthonya, J.T., Conaghanc, J., Ivanid, K., et al.: Computer-automated time-lapse analysis results correlate with embryo implantation and clinical pregnancy: a blinded, multi-centre study. Reprod. Biomed. Online **29**, 729–736 (2014). https://doi.org/10.1016/j.rbmo.2014.09.005
28. Santos Filho, E., Noble, J.A., Poli, M., Griffiths, T., Emerson, G., Wells, D.: A method for semi-automatic grading of human blastocyst microscope images. Hum. Reprod. **27**(9), 2641–2648 (2012). https://doi.org/10.1093/humrep/des219
29. Meyer, D., Leisch, F., Hornik, K.: The support vector machine under test. Neurocomputing **55**, 169–186 (2003). https://doi.org/10.1016/S0925-2312(03)00431-4

30. Ojala, T., Pietikainen, M., Maeenpaa, T.: Multiresolution gray-scale and rotation invariant texture classification with local binary patterns. IEEE Trans. Pattern Anal. Mach. Intell. 24, 971–987 (2002). https://doi.org/10.1109/TPAMI.2002.1017623
31. van Loendersloot, L., van Welya, M., van der Veena, F., Bossuyt, P., Repping, S.: Selection of embryos for transfer in IVF: ranking embryos based on their implantation potential using morphological scoring. Reprod. Biomed Online 29, 222–230 (2014). https://doi.org/10.1016/j.rbmo.2014.04.016
32. Chen, F., Neubourg, D.D., Debrock, S., Peeraer, K., D'Hooghe, T., Spiessens, C.: Selecting the embryo with the highest implantation potential using a data mining based prediction model. Reprod. Biol. Endocrinol. 14, 10 (2016). https://doi.org/10.1186/s12958-016-0145-1
33. Richardson, A., et al.: A clinically useful simplified blastocyst grading system. Reprod. Biomed. Online 31, 523–530 (2015). https://doi.org/10.1016/j.rbmo.2015.06.017
34. Takahashi, M.B., Rocha, J.C., Núñez, E.G.F.: Optimization of artificial neural network by genetic algorithm for describing viral production from uniform design data. Process Biochem. 51, 422–430 (2016). https://doi.org/10.1016/j.procbio.2015.12.005
35. Krogh, A.: What are artificial neural networks? Nat. Biotechnol. 26(2), 195–197 (2008). https://doi.org/10.1038/nbt1386
36. Tanomaru, J.: Motivação, fundamentos e aplicações de algoritmos genéticos. In: Proceedings of the II Congresso Brasileiros de Redes Neurais. II Escola de Redes Neurais, vol. 1, pp. 331–411 (1995)
37. Zhang, G., Patuwo, B.E., Hu, M.Y.: Forecasting with artificial neural networks: the state of the art. Int. J. Forecast. 14, 35–62 (1998). https://doi.org/10.1016/S0169-2070(97)00044-7
38. Huang, Y.: Advances in artificial neural networks - methodological development and application. Algorithms 2, 973–1007 (2009). https://doi.org/10.3390/algor2030973
39. Matos, F.D., Rocha, J.C., Nogueira, M.F.G.: A method using artificial neural networks to morphologically assess mouse blastocyst quality. J. Anim. Sci. Technol. 56, 15 (2014). https://doi.org/10.1186/2055-0391-56-15
40. Matos, F.D., Nogueira, M.F.G., Rocha, J.C.: Artificial intelligence meets the same challenges as humans in morphological classification of bovine blastocysts. Abstract of Proceedings of the 28th Annual Meeting of the Embryo Technology Society (SBTE), A209 Supporting Biotechnologies: Cryopreservation and Cryobiology, Image Analysis and Diagnosis, Molecular Biology and "Omics". Anim. Reprod. 11, 489 (2014)
41. Rocha, J.C., Passália, F.J., Matos, F.D., Takahashi, M.B., Ciniciato, D.S., et al.: A method based on artificial intelligence to fully automatize the evaluation of bovine blastocysts image. Sci. Rep. 7, 7659 (2017). https://doi.org/10.1038/s41598-017-08104-9
42. Rocha, J.C., Passália, F.J., Matos, F.D., Takahashi, M.B., Maserati Jr., M.P.: Automatized image processing of bovine blastocysts produced in vitro for quantitative variable determination. Sci. Data 4, 170192 (2017). https://doi.org/10.1038/sdata.2017.192
43. Atherton, T.J., Kerbyson, D.J.: Size invariant circle detection. Image Vis. Comput. 17, 795–803 (1999). https://doi.org/10.1016/S0262-8856(98)00160-7
44. Siqueira, F.R., Schwartz, W.R., Predrini, H.: Multi-scale level co-occurence matrices for texture description. Neutocomputing 120, 336–345 (2013). https://doi.org/10.1016/j.neucom.2012.09.042
45. Haralick, R.M., Shanmugam, K., Dinstein, I.: Textural features for image classification. IEEE Trans. System Man Cybern. 3, 610–621 (1973)
46. Hu, Y., Zhao, C., Wang, H.: Directional analysis of texture images using gray level co-occurrence matrix. In: IEEE Pacific-Asia Workshop on Computational Intelligence and Industrial Application, pp. 277–281 (2008). https://doi.org/10.1109/PACIIA.2008.279

47. Ludermir, T.B., Yamazaki, A., Zanchettin, C.: An optimization methodology for neural networks weights and architetures. IEEE Trans. Neural Netw. **17**, 1452–1459 (2006). https://doi.org/10.1109/TNN.2006.881047

48. Khosravi, A., Nahavandi, S., Creighton, D., Atiya, A.F.: Comprehensive review of neural network-based prediction intervals and new advances. IEEE Trans. Neural Netw. **22**, 1341–1356 (2011). https://doi.org/10.1109/TNN.2011.2162110

49. Ciniciato, D.S., Takahashi, M.B., Nogueira, M.F.G., Rocha, J.C.: Potential use of smartphone as a tool to capture embryo digital images from stereomicroscope and to evaluate them by an artificial neural network. In: Proceedings of the International Conference on Computer-Human Interaction Research and Applications (CHIRA), pp. 185–189 (2017). https://doi.org/10.5220/0006518501850189

50. Botigelli, R.C., et al.: Supplementing in vitro embryo production media by NPPC and sildenafil affect the cytoplasmic lipid content and gene expression of bovine cumulus-oocyte complexes and embryos. Reprod. Biol. **18**, 66–75 (2018). https://doi.org/10.1016/j.repbio.2018.01.004

Author Index

Printed in the United States
By Bookmasters